Internships
in Recreation and Leisure Services:
A Practical Guide for Students

BY

Edward E. Seagle, Jr., Ed.D.

Ralph W. Smith, Ph.D.

Lola M. Dalton, M.A.

Venture Publishing, Inc.
State College, PA

Printed in the United States of America

Library of Congress Cataloging in Publication Data
Seagle, Edward E., 1944–
    Internships in recreation and leisure services: A practical guide for students
Design/Illustration: Sandra Sikorski, Sikorski Design
Production: Bonnie Godbey
Printing and Binding: BookCrafters, Inc.

Library of Congress Catalogue Card Number 92-85021
ISBN 0-910251-55-X

10 9 8 7 6 5 4 3 2 1

NO TOC
ADDED SH.

Contents

Acknowledgements

The authors would like to thank the many people who helped to make this manual a reality, especially the faculty and students at California State University, Chico, and The Pennsylvania State University. The ideas, comments, contributions, and assistance of the following people deserve special recognition: James "Corky" Broughton, Murray State University; Steven Burr, The Pennsylvania State University; Judy Elliott, Lock Haven University; Robert Griffith, Pennsylvania Recreation and Parks Association; Frank Guadagnolo, The Pennsylvania State University; Deb Kerstetter, The Pennsylvania State University; Rod Warnick, University of Massachusetts; Tom Willson, Lock Haven University; and David Wood, National Recreation and Park Association. The authors would also like to express sincere appreciation to the staff at Venture Publishing, especially Bonnie Godbey, for the many hours of technical assistance they provided.

Aspects of the letters and resumes used in this text were modified from documents submitted by undergraduate students (now alumni) of California State University, Chico, and The Pennsylvania State University. These individuals include: Corinne Bauer, Brian Berry, Kimberly Berry-Kinahan, Kristy Bradford, Brenda Camp, Dana Christiansen, Christy Clark, Patricia Clayton, Lorie Coats, Kelly Craighead, Richard Dennison, Lisa Dieter, Debi Draper, Nic Draper, Andrew Fay, Claudine Gale, Todd Gordon, Beth Johnson, Nikki Keith, Jennifer McGlone, Suzanne McKechnie, Kris Mervine, Laurie Moberly-Williams, Karen Moretti, Dawn Mulberger, Clarice Nolan, Kimberly Oliver, Bruce Pace, Cecilia Peard, Cynthia Peters, Jacqueline Potter, Tracey Reinstein, Stacey Scott, Michael Seatter, Michael Shancez, Lorraine Shultz, Ann Sloan, Janine Smith, Anda Spalvins, Jennifer Trumbo, Michael Walker, Nancy Washwell, John Weissmuller, Gina Weitzel, Jane Wesbay, Leslie Williams, Leslie Witney, Judy Wood, Allyson Wreaks-Brennan, and Heidi Wulf-Walker.

Ed Seagle extends his personal thanks to his parents, Edward and Olive Seagle; wife Jeanne and family; co-workers, students and alumni at California State University, Chico; and his professional colleagues for their continued support. Also, a special thank you is extended to Buford Bush (Professor Emeritus) who appointed Dr. Seagle as Internship Coordinator at CSU, Chico, and the Recreation and Parks Management faculty members who have shown continued confidence in his performance as Internship Coordinator over the years.

Ralph Smith offers his personal thanks to his parents and family, especially his wife Tammy Buckley who assisted with every aspect of this project. In addition to Penn State's faculty, Dr. Smith would also like to recognize the contributions of colleagues who assisted him during his years at the University of Maryland, particularly Viki Annand, Jimmy Calloway (now at California State University, Northridge), Fred Humphrey, Seppo Iso-Ahola, and Veda Ward (now at California State University, Northridge).

Lola Dalton extends a special thank you to her colleagues in the Career Planning and Placement Center at California State University, Chico, for taking the time to listen to her suggestions and for positive feedback.

INTRODUCTION

"Success is a journey, not a destination."
—Ben Sweetland

You are approaching one of the most important academic decisions of your college years: selecting an internship site in recreation and leisure services. A good internship brings academic coursework to life, and provides work experiences and professional contacts that help ensure a successful professional career. Your internship is the foundation for your future . . . and like any strong foundation, its construction requires time, effort and the proper tools. The purpose of this text is to give you the proper tools for getting the best possible internship—the time and effort are up to you, however.

Before charging ahead, it is important to acknowledge some thoughts that many students have as they approach the internship search. These include:

- "My GPA isn't very strong, so I probably won't be offered the best internships."

- "I don't feel ready for entering the work environment. Maybe I need to take more courses."

- "I don't have a lot of work experience in leisure services, so why would an internship site want me?"

- "It's not *what* you know, but *who* you know that counts . . . and I don't know *anybody*!"

- "I don't even know where to *start* looking for an internship site."

Many college students are uncertain about their qualifications and career readiness, and most have some degree of anxiety about the future. Feelings of uncertainty and anxiety are normal, particularly when you are confronted with an important decision like internship selection. Hopefully, as you progress through this manual, any uncertainties or anxieties you presently feel will fade and be replaced by the confidence that comes from doing a thorough job of preparation. Students who know the most people, have the best GPAs, or accumulate the most work experiences aren't necessarily the ones selected by an internship site. Rather, internships are usually awarded to students who have taken the time to prepare, in detail, for their internship selection.

Without being aware of it, you have been preparing for your internship for years. People you have met, things you have done, and information you have collected throughout your life are all helpful in identifying and securing an internship. In the chapters that follow, you will be going through a systematic internship selection process that will help you utilize your life experiences and available resources to maximum advantage. The ultimate goal is to help you identify and secure an internship that not only meets your academic objectives, but also enhances your professional career in recreation and leisure services. The internship selection process includes:

(1)   conducting a thorough self-assessment;
(2)   determining your direction, including setting internship goals;
(3)   searching for appropriate agencies and researching the most promising ones;
(4)   preparing to contact agencies, including cover letters and resumes;
(5)   preparing for and participating in interviews; and
(6)   deciding which intern site is best for you.

The above steps are covered in detail in this manual. Each chapter: (1) presents information for you to read and think about; (2) includes exercises for you to complete; and (3) lists, whenever appropriate, pertinent questions for you to ponder. Overall, the intent of the manual is to help you develop effective internship tools and refine your internship selection process. Throughout the manual, we have tried to include examples from a variety of recreation and leisure service specializations (e.g., outdoor recreation, therapeutic recreation, commercial recreation) to illustrate important points and concepts.

As you begin to read the chapters that follow, it is essential to remember that your department's internship coordinator is a critical link in your internship selection process. Each college and university has its own procedures and policies related to internships in recreation and leisure services; therefore, prior to finalizing *each* step of the internship selection process outlined in this manual, you should consult with your internship coordinator and, if appropriate, your academic advisor.

Students With Disabilities

Persons with disabilities are encouraged to order *Career Development Guide for Professionals with Disabilities* as a supplement to this manual. This annual guide focuses on job seeking skills and career development issues for persons with disabling conditions. It is available (nominal charge) from:

CRS Recruitment Publications
1800 Sherman Place
Evanston, IL 60201
(708) 475-8800)

Appendix D also cites some career-related publications written for persons with disabilities.

CHAPTER ONE

Self-Assessment

"The spirit of self-help is the root of all genuine growth in the individual."
—Samuel Smiles

This chapter is intended to assist you in identifying who you are and what you have to offer a potential internship agency. We will help you examine your own self-confidence, personal philosophy, personality traits, professional skills, limitations, and attitude toward work. In so doing, we hope to assist you to look back at your history/development and identify those things that have helped you to become a unique human being. Examining yourself and your past is essential because all of your life experiences help determine how you will approach your career choices. Self-exploration will help you to reach the internship and career goals you set. Knowledge is power, and an in-depth evaluation of yourself will provide the knowledge you need to assume power over your professional life.

In this chapter you will examine your own:

• Self-Confidence

• Personal Philosophy

• Interests and Needs

• Personality Traits and Professional Skills

• Limitations and Weakness

• Attitudes Toward Work and Learning

Self-Confidence

First, it is important to take a look at how you feel about your own abilities. If you believe in yourself, you are likely to have positive feelings about yourself *and* project a positive image to others. Since this is so important to your professional future, you need to take some time to assess your self-confidence. Specifically, you need to identify those positive and negative statements (internal messages) that you make to yourself. It is especially important to take note of any negative statements and find ways to change them into positive statements.

Ask yourself the following questions. Each "yes" answer indicates that you are enhancing your own self-confidence and projecting a *positive* image to others.

Do you:

- REGULARLY GIVE YOURSELF POSITIVE STROKES FOR ACCOMPLISHMENTS?
  Examples include the following internal messages to yourself: I did a good job preparing my resume." "When I made that presentation, I displayed confidence and spoke with authority." "Way to go! I deserve congratulations on completing that assignment."

- USE POSITIVE SELF-TALK WHEN YOU APPROACH A CHALLENGE?
  Examples include: "I am confident in my abilities to perform this internship." "I have what it takes to succeed in this internship." "I have confidence in my interviewing skills." "During this interview I will be on top, in control, and successful."

- USE POSITIVE BODY LANGUAGE WHEN INTERACTING WITH OTHERS?
  Examples include: displaying good sitting and standing posture; maintaining eye contact; using appropriate gestures to emphasize points.

- USE YOUR VOICE EFFECTIVELY WHEN COMMUNICATING YOUR THOUGHTS?
  Examples include: speaking in a clear and resonant voice; varying your inflection to maintain interest and emphasize important points; pronouncing words distinctly and with authority.

Now, ask yourself the following questions. Each "yes" answer may mean that you are doing things to undermine your own self-confidence and project a *negative* image to others.

Do you:

- REGULARLY GIVE YOURSELF CRITICISM FOR THINGS YOU DO OR MISTAKES YOU MAKE?
  Examples include the following internal messages to yourself: Your resume looks like an elementary school child's." "How could you be so stupid as to forget the answer to that question?" "There you go, messing things up again!" "You should have known better than to try that."

- USE NEGATIVE SELF-TALK WHEN YOU APPROACH A CHALLENGE?
  Examples include: "I can't do this job." "I'm not good enough to get selected for an interview." "I did not get the last internship, so I will not get this one." "I shouldn't even bother to try, it's too difficult for me."

- RATIONALIZE OR MINIMIZE YOUR SUCCESSES?
  Examples include: "I don't deserve such a good internship." "The only reason I got an interview is because I am a minority student." "If it hadn't been for the help other people gave me, I never could have developed a decent resume." "Sure, I got the internship, but the competition wasn't very tough."

Throughout the next week, analyze your own internal messages. Is your self-talk positive or negative? Do you give yourself credit for the good things that you do, or do you rationalize or minimize your accomplishments. If you find that you are giving negative messages to yourself, you need to work hard toward changing them. This can be done by:

(1) being attuned to your own self-talk,

(2) recognizing when a negative message is beginning,

(3) interrupting your own negative message *as soon as it starts,* and

(4) consciously substituting positive self-talk in place of your negative message.

Changing your self-talk is not easy. It is hard work, but it is well worth the effort. There are many examples of people who succeeded against difficult odds (see box), and most of them did so because they wouldn't allow negative self-talk to get in their way. By giving yourself positive messages, you will be able to get the maximum from *your* abilities.

Examples of Positive Thinking

Take a look at the following examples of people who succeeded in overcoming difficult challenges. True, these people had exceptional talent . . . but they probably wouldn't have succeeded without the self-confidence that comes from positive strokes and positive self-talk.

- Althea Gibson, as a young African-American in Harlem, believing she could be the first black tennis champion at Wimbledon.

- Neil Armstrong believing he could make his mark in aviation.

- Stevie Wonder believing he could enlighten people's lives through music.

- O. J. Simpson believing he could break Jim Brown's professional football rushing record.

- Walter Payton believing he could improve on O. J.'s record.

- Sally Ride believing she could become the first woman astronaut.

- Rick Hansen, a Canadian wheelchair athlete, believing he could wheel around the world in his wheelchair. Upon returning from his successful "Man in Motion" tour around the world, he was greeted by over 50,000 people.

- Mary Lou Retton, U.S. Olympic gymnastics gold medalist in the 1984 Olympic games in Los Angeles, believing she could get the perfect 10 she needed to win.

- George Burns, on the occasion of his 90th birthday, believing that, "I can't die, I'm booked."

Personal Philosophy

A personal philosophy of life is something we all have, but many people have not thought about their own philosophy long enough to define it clearly. Understanding *your* personal philosophy is important because it gives you an advantage in an internship interview and, later, guides your search for fulfilling employment in recreation and leisure services. A sound personal philosophy allows you to describe who you are and what life means to you. It also provides direction in your life by helping you recognize what things are important to you.

In order to examine your personal philosophy it helps to conduct a review of your life: How did you arrive at this point in your life? What life experiences have had a major impact upon your life? Who are the friends and relatives who have had an influence upon your life? What beliefs do you share with these individuals? What heroes have you had while growing up? What was it about their lives that made them heroes to you? Take a moment to reflect on these questions. The ultimate purpose of a life review is to help you answer this question: What *fundamental* concepts do you value most and use to guide your life's direction?

Once you have identified the concepts that are most important to you, you will be better able to answer fundamental questions about your professional future. The questions include: Where do you see your professional life heading? What do you see as your eventual career and how do you plan to get there? How do you define professional "success?"

EXERCISE TIME!

At this point, complete the exercise in Figure 1.1. By writing a one-page narrative describing your personal philosophy of life, you should understand yourself better . . . and you should get a better understanding of where you want to go with your professional life.

Figure 1.1
Personal Philosophy Statement

Use this page (and additional paper, if needed) to describe your personal philosophy of life. Feel free to brainstorm—just let your thoughts go. After all, there are no right or wrong answers when expressing your own philosophy of life.

Once you have finished your personal philosophy statement, review it. Look for key words that *best* express your personal view of life. After you have identified these key words, circle them (or highlight them using a color marking pen). Do these key words indicate anything pertaining to your professional career? If so, write down how these words relate to your career.

Interests and Needs

Soon, you will be required to make a very important and perhaps difficult decision—where to do your internship. In order to make this decision, you should have a good understanding of your own personal and professional interests and needs. What aspects of your personal and professional life add to your happiness? What leisure interests do you have? How important are they to you? What is it about a particular career or job that makes you interested in pursuing it? How important is it for you to work with creative people, to work for an understanding boss, to make a lot of money, to be able to upgrade your skills, to achieve promotions, to live in a small city, to live in a safe community, etc.? These questions, and others like them, are important to ask yourself *before* you embark on your professional career. They will help you understand what things you need and want from both your personal and professional lives. Meeting your needs and interests may be essential in order for you to continue to be productive in your career and achieve the "success" you are seeking. Later, in Chapter Three, you will have a chance to analyze how well prospective internship sites meet your personal and professional needs.

Personality Traits and Professional Skills

As an applicant for an internship position, you need to know your own personality, as well as your professional skills and potential. Over the years, you have developed a wide variety of skills, and each internship supervisor has requirements that must be matched to the skills of prospective interns. If you are to do an effective job of selling yourself to a potential internship supervisor, you must have a thorough understanding of your own personal and professional strengths. By knowing your strengths, you will be able to emphasize them during the application and interview process. Take this opportunity to examine yourself and your skills and potential.

The next few pages provide exercises to help you assess your professional skills and potential, as well as your own personality traits. When completing these exercises, it is essential to be honest! You might also ask others close to you to review these forms and provide input. Sometimes others seem to know us better than we know ourselves. It is also important that you take your time completing these exercises. If they are done in haste, you will not receive the maximum benefit from them. These exercises are intended to help you know yourself, and knowing yourself well is the cornerstone to building a successful professional career.

EXERCISE TIME!

The next exercise is a "Personal and Professional Assessment" (Figure 1.2). Use this form to list your past and present work experiences and some skills you have acquired from each position. Also, list some academic skills that you have gained in school and some personality traits that you possess. This exercise is open-ended; that is, it allows you to choose descriptions of yourself and your abilities. Once you have completed this exercise, turn to the next two pages (Figures 1.3 and 1.4) and complete the Professional Skills Assessment and Personality Traits Assessment. These checklists should help you expand your awareness of traits and skills that are important for a student intern to possess.

Figure 1.2
Personal and Professional Assessment

This sheet is designed to assist you in examining your own skills, achievements, and personality traits/skills. *Reflect* on what professional and academic skills you have developed and what personality characteristics you demonstrate. Be honest and thorough in this self-evaluation. Use additional paper, if needed.

A. PROFESSIONAL ASSESSMENT

EXPERIENCE (Paid or Volunteer)   YOUR SKILLS AND ACHIEVEMENTS

1. _____   1. _____

2. _____   2. _____

3. _____   3. _____

4. _____   4. _____

5. _____   5. _____

6. _____   6. _____

B. EDUCATIONAL ASSESSMENT

What relevant skills and knowledge have I gained from my academic studies?

1. _____

2. _____

3. _____

4. _____

5. _____

6. _____

7. _____

8. _____

Figure 1.3
Professional Skills Assessment

Listed below are a variety of professional skills which may be important for you to demonstrate during your internship and throughout your professional career.

This form can be used to: (1) identify specific professional skills you possess, plus those you need to refine or acquire; or (2) assess whether your skills match the requirements of the specific internship position you are seeking.

This list does not include all possible professional skills. Feel free to add any additional professional skills that you want to assess, especially those important to your professional specialization or option.

Internship Position Title (Optional) _____

Professional Skills	I Already Possess	I Already Possess, But Need To Refine	I Need To Acquire	Not Needed For Internship
Advising				
Analyzing				
Assessing				
Budgeting				
Communicating (written)				
Communicating (oral)				
Computing				
Conceptualizing				
Consulting				
Coordinating				
Decision Making				
Delegating				
Designing				
Directing				
Documenting				
Evaluating				
Goal Setting				
Initiating				
Instructing				
Leading				
Managing				
Marketing				
Negotiating				
Observing				
Organizing				
Planning				
Problem Solving				
Reporting				
Scheduling				
Selling				
Supervising				
Teaching				
Team Building				
Writing				

Figure 1.4
Personality Traits Assessment

Listed below are a variety of personality traits/skills which may be important for you to demonstrate during your internship and throughout your professional career.

This form can be used to: (1) identify specific personality traits/skills you possess, plus those you need to refine or acquire; or (2) assess whether your traits/skills match the requirements of the specific internship position you are seeking.

This list does not include all possible personality traits/skills. Feel free to add any additional traits/skills that you want to assess, especially those important to your professional specialization or option.

Internship Position Title (Optional) _____

Personality Traits/Skills	I Already Am	I Already Am, But Need To Refine	I Need To Become	Not Needed For Internship
Able to laugh freely				
Able to say no				
Accepting of criticism				
Communicative				
Confident				
Considerate of others				
Cooperative				
Creative				
Determined				
Dynamic				
Empathetic				
Enthusiastic				
Flexible				
Friendly				
Good listener				
Hard worker				
Honest				
Intelligent				
Loyal				
Motivated				
Open-Minded				
Patient				
Poised				
Punctual				
Proud				
Reflective				
Reliable				
Resourceful				
Responsible				
Risk-Taker				
Self-Reliant				
Spontaneous				
Stable (emotionally)				
Tactfulness				

Limitations/Weaknesses

Everyone has limitations, and it is important for you to be aware of your personal and professional weaknesses. By knowing your limitations, you will be able to work toward overcoming them. The preceding sections and exercises focused upon identifying your strengths, but they also enabled you to assess areas of weakness. Return to Figures 1.3 and 1.4 and identify the skills or traits that you need to refine or acquire. Are any of these skills or traits important to success in the type of internship you are seeking? If so, you need to develop a specific plan for overcoming these limitations. During the weeks ahead, set goals that will help you eliminate or diminish these limitations. For example, if you are often late to classes or work, set a *reasonable* goal for next week (e.g., only being late twice during the week). If you do not achieve your goal during the first week, keep the goal the same and increase your determination to achieve it. If you *do* achieve your goal for the first week, raise your expectations for the next week, and so on. Establishing reasonable goals and working hard to achieve them can turn limitations into assets.

Attitudes Toward Work and Learning

Most internship supervisors mention a student's attitude toward work and learning as being a major factor in their evaluation of the student's performance. Having a positive attitude toward work includes being committed to the position and the agency, understanding and following the agency's philosophy, and being dedicated to the delivery of services and products that benefit the agency. Internship supervisors are looking for students who will carry out and follow through on assigned duties, work well independently *and* with others, and be on time and eager to learn from their work experiences.

The attitudes you display toward work and learning during your internship will help determine:

(1)   how other interns and coworkers feel about you;

(2)   how well you rate on internship evaluations;

(3)   what type of employment reference letter you will receive after graduation; and

(4)   how much consideration you will receive for any future job opening with your internship agency.

EXERCISE TIME!

It is vital to establish and continue to demonstrate a positive attitude toward work and toward *learning* while you are at work. The following page (Figure 1.5) offers you a chance to develop your own "Work and Learning Attitude Profile." Take the time to write down what you intend to do on your internship that will demonstrate your positive attitude.

Figure 1.5
Work and Learning Attitude Profile

Reflect on what you are willing to commit to your internship agency. What specific things do you intend to do during your internship that will demonstrate your commitment to the agency, your interest in learning, and your dedication to the quality of your work? In the space below, make a list of the actions and behaviors that will demonstrate your *positive* attitude toward work and learning.

SUMMARY

Chapter One forms the foundation for an effective internship search and a successful internship experience. It provided you with information and exercises to examine your own personal and professional qualities. Once you have mastered the information in this chapter, you can move ahead with confidence because you have created a sound cornerstone for your internship experience. Knowledge of yourself provides baseline information for establishing internship and career goals, developing a high-quality cover letter and resume, and preparing for a successful internship interview. Now it is time to move ahead by exploring what *you* want to get from your internship and your professional career.

CHAPTER TWO

Direction

"People with goals succeed because they know where they're going."
—Earl Nightingale

"In the struggle to reach your goals, there is only one way to move—forward."
—Maxwell Maltz

This chapter will help you set internship and career goals to get your career on the right track, and help to keep it there. Setting goals is crucial because these goals will provide the direction you need to make sound career-related decisions. You might think of this chapter as a road map to your professional future—it enables you to plan your route to success and, along the way, it serves to keep you on your desired course.

In this chapter, you will identify your internship and
career direction by establishing:

• Internship Goals

• Career Goals

• Action Plan Time Line

INTERNSHIP/CAREER DIRECTION

Even before preparing your resume or seeking information on internship agencies, it is time to give serious consideration to what you are looking for in your internship and in your professional career. You should ask yourself a few basic questions that will help to clarify your internship and career direction.

EXERCISE TIME!

The following pages (Figure 2.1) give you a chance to answer some of these questions and to evaluate how your answers provide direction to your internship and career. At this point, turn the page and complete Figure 2.1.

Figure 2.1
Internship/Career Direction Exercise

Part I. Questions

For each question below, write your *answer* in the space provided. Then, go back to each question and write down the *direction* (i.e., type of agency and work experiences) your answer suggests you should take to pursue a successful internship and career.

1. "What career experiences do I have to build upon?"

    Answer:

    Direction:

2. "At this point, what important career experiences do I lack?"

    Answer:

    Direction:

3. "What type of work do I enjoy most?"

    Answer:

    Direction:

Figure 2.1 (continued)
Internship/Career Direction Exercise

4. "Ultimately, what kind of professional position do I want to have?"

    Answer:

    Direction:

5. "What employment choices are viable for me upon graduation?"

    Answer:

    Direction:

Part II.
Internship and Career Direction

Review what you have written above. Then, based upon your *answers* and the *direction* each answer provides, indicate the *ultimate* direction you think your internship and career should take.

Internship Goals

Once you have clarified the direction of your internship and professional career, it is time to establish some concrete goals for your internship. Almost every written success story includes statements about the value of setting clear and concise goals. Goals allow you to identify exactly what you want to learn and help you to establish a path for goal attainment. Internship goals, however, do even more than that. When shared with your university's faculty and your agency supervisor, internship goals enable these important people to tailor your internship responsibilities and learning opportunities to fit *your* unique needs and interests.

Students sometimes ask us how they can prepare a list of goals *before* they select their internship site. In fact, it is essential to prepare goals in advance so that you can select a site that offers the kinds of experiences and learning opportunities you need. After you start the internship, you and your agency supervisor should revise your goals slightly, based upon agency requirements. However, be sure that most of your internship goals are achievable at the agency you select.

Internship goals can also serve as an unofficial "contract" that assures you will be taught the work-related skills you need for success in your profession. Ultimately, your primary internship goal is to learn, through experience, as much as possible during your internship. However, it is important to identify *specific* experiences and learning opportunities that you want to have during your internship. Your internship goals should focus upon both what you want to learn (skills and knowledge) and how you want to learn it (experiences). Take time to think realistically about your goals. What things will you be able to learn in the time available? What duties and responsibilities are available to a student intern? What are the essential entry-level skills in your area of specialization? Then, using the information below, develop a comprehensive list of goals that will guide your internship site selection and give specific direction to your internship experience.

Writing Internship Goals

Goals, as used in this manual, are general outcome statements. They specify what you expect to learn and to experience during your internship. Goals are not as specific as "objectives," and they are not necessarily observable and measurable. They must, however, be specific enough to allow you and your supervisor to assess whether or not you are achieving your goals. The information that follows should help you to prepare a comprehensive list of goals for your internship.

(1) Include generic skills that are important to any recreation and leisure service professional. These include leadership skills, interpersonal skills, administrative skills, etc.

(2) Identify entry-level skills that are important in your area of specialization. For example, a commercial recreation student's goals may include marketing, selling, and accounting skills, whereas a therapeutic recreation student's goals might include skills related to assessment, documentation, and leisure education.

(3) Build upon skills you already possess and identify skills that you need to obtain. Refer to Figure 2.1, Questions 1 and 2 on page 16 to help you.

(4) Whenever possible, include verbs that clarify what you actually plan to *do,* rather than focusing exclusively on what you want to learn. For example, you may be able to learn by observing your supervisor lead activities. However, you would learn *more* by actually leading activities yourself.

(5) Be comprehensive. Make sure that all *essential* entry-level skills are covered in your list of goals. You do not want to realize, too late, that your internship did not include experiences that are vital to securing a job after graduation.

(6) Be realistic. Do not include experiences that would *not* be attainable or available during an internship. For example, a student intern would not actually *prepare* a departmental budget. However, he or she should able to learn how the budgeting process works.

Examples of Internship Goals

Carefully review the lists of internship goals provided on the next four pages (20-23). We have included examples from a variety of specializations. Therefore, not all of these goals will be appropriate for your career direction. Use these examples for guidance, but be sure to write your goals with *your* experiences and career direction in mind. Also, use your own style and wording when writing goal statements.

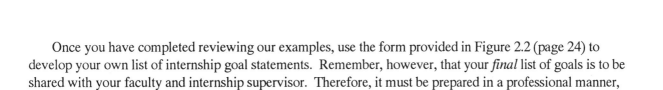

EXERCISE TIME!

Once you have completed reviewing our examples, use the form provided in Figure 2.2 (page 24) to develop your own list of internship goal statements. Remember, however, that your *final* list of goals is to be shared with your faculty and internship supervisor. Therefore, it must be prepared in a professional manner, using a typewriter or computer.

INTERNSHIP GOALS—EXAMPLE #1

Mei Chung

During my internship, I would like to:

1. select, implement, and evaluate treatment, leisure education and recreation participation services for clientele;

2. accurately and effectively assess clients' leisure-related needs;

3. develop therapeutic recreation plans with goals and objectives for individual clientele based on assessment;

4. serve as a part of an interdisciplinary team and become knowledgeable about treatment methods and techniques of other allied health disciplines;

5. document client progress regularly, accurately and efficiently, modifying therapeutic recreation plans as needed;

6. accurately document each assigned client's status at discharge;

7. gain a greater understanding of the agency and clientele by attending workshops and in-service sessions, with particular emphasis upon disabling conditions;

8. understand administrative processes utilized in managing a therapeutic recreation facility including budgeting, reimbursement procedures, staff management, and scheduling; and

9. increase my awareness of laws, regulations, and accreditation standards that affect the agency and its clientele.

INTERNSHIP GOALS—EXAMPLE #2

Robert A. Benson

My internship goals are to:

1. gain knowledge of the administrative operation within the agency and the responsibilities of the staff;

2. develop an understanding of the various financial procedures and budgeting techniques utilized by the agency;

3. organize, plan, and implement recreation/leisure programs that will effectively meet the needs of the individuals served;

4. develop quality public relations with staff members and the agency's clientele by demonstrating effective interpersonal skills;

5. accurately and efficiently evaluate recreation/leisure programs within the agency;

6. gain direct experience with promotional efforts utilized by the agency, including methods used to channel these efforts to potential clientele;

7. develop an understanding of maintenance procedures involved in efficiently operating the agency's facilities;

8. learn the appropriate procedures for operating concession and vending amenities within the agency by directly assisting in these operations;

9. demonstrate the ability to solve problems common to a commercial recreation operation;

10. learn effective methods and procedures for management of human resources in a commercial recreation operation, including hiring practices, termination policies, staff evaluation, and in-service training arrangements;

11. gain an understanding of risk management procedures utilized by the agency; and

12. gain an appreciation of the qualities needed to be an effective and efficient manager within a commercial operation.

INTERNSHIP GOALS—EXAMPLE #3

Rebecca Thompson

During my internship, I would like to:

1.   learn about the financial aspects involved in operating a public recreation agency, including budgeting and program fee determination;

2.   learn about the administration of an agency by directly assisting with the duties and responsibilities of the administrator, supervisor, and program director;

3.   better understand the overall impact of legal liabilities on a public recreation agency;

4.   gain experience in the preparation of a budget for various recreation programs and for a recreation agency;

5.   assist with the implementation of an effective public relations strategy within the agency and in the community;

6.   plan and conduct various recreation programs for a variety of age groups;

7.   create and assist with the distribution of publicity materials for agency programs;

8.   learn how to create an efficient and effective overall schedule of programs for a public recreation agency; and

9.   construct and implement an evaluation tool to determine if selected programs are meeting stated goals and objectives.

INTERNSHIP GOALS—EXAMPLE #4

Althea Brown

My internship goals are to:

1. use survey methodology to identify outdoor recreation needs and interests of a wide diversity of individuals and groups;

2. evaluate the degree to which outdoor recreation programs are meeting their established goals and objectives;

3. observe and directly participate in three areas of the agency: resource management, administration, and interpretation;

4. better understand the interrelationship between environment/wildlife and human beings, with emphasis upon management techniques that are mutually beneficial;

5. be involved with agency-related resource management projects such as wildlife inventories, trail maintenance, and patrol and vegetation surveys;

6. demonstrate effective public relations skills by interacting with the public and agency staff in an effective and courteous manner;

7. understand the administration of outdoor programs with emphasis upon the budgeting, staff relations, public relations, and personnel supervision;

8. gain an understanding of facility layout, daily operations, maintenance, equipment and supplies;

9. learn about the policies and practices of other recreation and park agencies in the local geographic area by visiting at least three facilities;

10. become aware of the implications of the state and federal laws and regulations related to outdoor recreation agencies; and

11. observe supervisory techniques of selected outdoor recreation professionals to help me become an effective supervisor.

Figure 2.2
Internship Goals

In the space provided, develop *at least* eight (8) goals that you want to accomplish during your internship experience. Be sure that these goals conform to the information provided in this chapter.

Goal #1: _____

_____

_____

Goal #2: _____

_____

_____

Goal #3: _____

_____

_____

Goal #4: _____

_____

_____

Goal #5: _____

_____

_____

Goal #6: _____

_____

_____

Goal #7: _____

_____

_____

Goal #8: _____

_____

_____

Career Goals

Although internship goals are your primary concern at this point in your professional life, it is also important to formulate some career goals. Earlier in this chapter, you answered some questions that helped to provide information about your career direction. Now, you should take the time to develop some career goals that will provide direction for internship selection. As was true of internship goals, career goals should be general outcome statements; however, they are longer range than internship goals and should indicate a progression as you move across your career path.

EXERCISE TIME!

Figure 2.3 provides a form to help you develop some career goals. Using this form, state an overall career goal (what you hope to accomplish during your career) and develop 5-year and 10- to 15-year goals to help you accomplish your overall career goal. After you have completed Figure 2.3, check to make sure your career goals are consistent with your career direction information in Figure 2.1 (pages 16-17). If not, you may want to revise your goals or reconsider your career direction.

Figure 2.3
Career Goals

Use the space provided to develop a workable set of goals for your professional career. Be as specific as possible.

OVERALL CAREER GOAL STATEMENT

Area of Development	5 Year Goal	10- to 15-Year Goal
Work Environment		
Specific Job Title		
Duties/Responsibilities		
Salary Range		
Benefits		

Action Plan Time Line

So far in this chapter, you have identified your internship goals and some career goals. It is now time to develop your "action plan" for getting the best possible internship—one that will enable you to meet your internship goals *and* get you started toward accomplishing your career goals. In effect, this manual is your internship action plan. It begins with a self-assessment (Chapter One) and systematically takes you through the steps necessary for you to get the internship you want.

At this point, it is important to begin looking ahead to the things you have left to accomplish *before* starting your internship. The best way to do this is by use of an action plan "time line." Constructing and using your time line involves four steps. These are:

(1)   Identify all internship-related tasks you need to do between now and when you start your internship.

(2)   Arrange these tasks in the order you need to *start* them, beginning with setting your internship goals and progressing through to the start of your internship.

(3)   Use backward planning techniques to establish deadline dates. These include "target" dates for finishing each task, and "starting" dates by which you need to begin working on the task in order to complete it on time. Beginning at the *end* of your list, place a "target" date on your last item. Then, estimate how long it will take to complete the task. Some tasks can be completed on the same day, while others may take weeks to complete. Repeat this process for each task working your way from the bottom of the list to the top. Be sure to set *realistic* dates for each task.

(4)   Record your "completion" date for each task. This is the *actual* date you completed the task. By monitoring your starting dates and comparing your completion date with the target date, you can easily keep track of your progress.

In developing your time line, there are some important things to consider. First, allow plenty of time to accomplish each task. Also, while it is important to stay on schedule, you also must remain flexible with many of your target dates. Murphy's Law reminds us that "if anything can go wrong, it will." Thus, you need to be prepared for some setbacks and don't panic if you miss a target date or two. Keep in mind, however, that some dates are *not* flexible. Examples of inflexible target dates may include your deadline for notifying university personnel of your internship selection and the starting date of your internship.

EXERCISE TIME!

Figure 2.4 provides a sample time line with starting and target dates. Review this example, and then construct one of your own using Figure 2.5.

Figure 2.4
Sample Time Line

Task	Starting Date	Target Date	Completion Date
1. Develop internship and career goals	Jan. 22	Jan. 25	_____
2. Compile list of potential internship agencies	Jan. 25	Feb. 12	_____
3. Discuss potential agencies with appropriate faculty	Feb. 15	Feb. 19	_____
4. Research information on potential agencies	Feb. 19	Mar. 12	_____
5. Prepare cover letter	Feb. 19	Feb. 22	_____
6. Construct resume	Feb. 22	Mar. 5	_____
7. Review resume with appropriate faculty	Mar. 8	Mar. 9	_____
8. Revise cover letter and resume	Mar. 10	Mar. 12	_____
9. Decide which agencies to pursue	Mar. 15	Mar. 15	_____
10. Mail cover letters and resumes to selected agencies	Mar. 17	Mar. 19	_____
11. Make follow-up phone calls to establish interview dates	Mar. 29	Mar. 31	_____
12. Confirm interview dates/times in writing	Apr. 1	Apr. 2	_____
13. Participate in interviews	Apr. 17	Apr. 24	_____
14. Send "thank you" letter to interviewers	Apr. 22	Apr. 26	_____
15. Select internship site	Apr. 9	Apr. 9	_____
16. Discuss selection with appropriate faculty	Apr. 12	Apr. 14	_____
17. Confirm arrangements with internship supervisor (starting date, housing arrangements, stipend, etc.)	Apr. 16	Apr. 16	_____
18. Notify other agencies of internship selection	Apr. 26	Apr. 30	_____
19. Register for internship credits at university	May 3	May 3	_____
20. Travel to internship site	May 20	May 22	_____
21. Move into internship housing	May 22	May 22	_____
22. Begin internship	May 24	May 24	_____

Figure 2.5
Internship Time Line

Task	Starting Date	Target Date	Completion Date

SUMMARY

Preparing for making decisions and taking action is an important aspect of your internship selection process. A well-conceived action plan, based on sound internship and career goals, is the catalyst for a successful internship experience.

This chapter helped you to develop a clear picture of what you want to achieve from your internship, and it is now time to explore how best to achieve these goals. The search process described in Chapter Three will give you concrete examples of how to begin identifying agencies that will enable you to meet your internship goals.

Search and Research

"If there's a way to do it better . . . find it."
—Thomas Edison

"The contact you are looking for might be as close as the next person you meet."
—Edward Seagle

This chapter will help you search for and identify potential internship agencies. Searching for an internship agency can be a frustrating and time-consuming process. A thorough search is well worth the effort, however. If you are systematic and thorough in your search for an internship site, you will end up with the best possible internship—one that helps *you* accomplish your career goals. This chapter is intended to help you search for and identify potential internship sites. Once you have identified some potential agencies, the chapter will give you guidelines for researching each of these agencies in depth.

To conduct a systematic search for internship agencies you will:

• Identify *essential characteristics* of potential agencies;

• Determine your *own needs and preferences* for an internship site;

• *Prioritize* your needs and preferences;

• Identify *resources* for information on agencies meeting essential characteristics; and

• Compile a "short list" of *potential agencies* that meet essential characteristics and correspond with your needs and preferences.

SEARCH

The first step in searching for an internship site is to decide what types of agencies or organizations would meet your needs. The preceding chapters have helped you to examine yourself and your career direction. Now, you must identify potential internship sites that offer the experiences you need or want.

It is important to keep in mind that your search process does not need to include time consuming, in-depth examination of each potential agency. That will come later; for now, just concentrate upon getting enough information to reduce your alternatives to a manageable number (i.e., 5 to 8 agencies).

Search Step #1:
Identify Essential Characteristics of Agencies

You should begin your search process by: (1) determining the type of agency or organization that corresponds with your professional interests, and (2) considering your requirements regarding geographic location of the agency or organization. In the next step, we will provide you with a list of other considerations to help narrow your alternatives, but at first it is important to keep your search as *broad* as possible.

Type of Agency or Organization

First, of course, you probably want to identify sites that offer leisure services corresponding with your option or emphasis area (i.e., Commercial Recreation, Outdoor Recreation, etc.). You should also consider whether or not you need an internship offering a specific specialization within your option. For example, you may be studying Outdoor Recreation and specializing in historical interpretation. For you, an essential characteristic of any agency is that it provides historical interpretive services. Or, you may be planning to work in Therapeutic Recreation, specializing in physical rehabilitation. You would, therefore, need to identify organizations that have certified TR specialists and offer physical rehabilitation services. Make sure, however, that any specialization you identify is *essential* to your professional goals. If you have a preference for a given specialization, but it is not essential, consider it in Step #2 of the search process.

Geographic Location of Agency or Organization

Many students feel limited by geographic considerations. Due to family constraints, interpersonal relationships, financial considerations, preferences for certain climates, etc., they want to confine their search for an internship site to a specific city, state, or region of the country. It is important to remember, however, that this step in the search process focuses on *essential* characteristics of agencies. If you are preparing for a career in ski resort management, for example, limiting your search to cold weather climates is essential. Moreover, a few universities require that an internship be confined to a specific region or state. However, some factors that seem essential may not be. For example, financial need may be overcome with an internship that pays a

salary. Before limiting *your* internship search to a specific geographic area, try to make sure that this limitation really is *essential.* If it is not essential, give it consideration in Step #2 of the search process.

Once you have identified essential characteristics of a potential internship agency, list these on the "Internship Selection Priority Form" (Figure 3.3) on page 38.

Search Step #2:
Determine Your Own Needs and Preferences

This stage of the search process focuses upon identifying and prioritizing your: (1) profession-related internship needs and preferences, and (2) personal internship needs and preferences. You should identify as many needs and preferences as possible.

Profession-related Needs and Preferences

The first two chapters of this manual helped you identify your own personal and professional strengths and weaknesses, as well as career direction and interests. Now this information will be helpful in determining your own internship needs and preferences. Return to these two chapters and review each of the exercises that you completed. In addition to reviewing these exercises, some additional questions need to be answered regarding your profession-related needs and preferences.

EXERCISE TIME!

By completing the "Profession-related Needs and Preferences Form" (Figure 3.1) on the next page, you will help to clarify some specific needs and preferences that your internship should provide.

Figure 3.1
Profession-related Needs and Preferences Form

The following list of questions will help you identify factors to consider when selecting potential internship agencies. Check "yes" or "no" depending upon your own *profession-related* needs or preferences:

1. Do I need a nearby university for supervision or coursework?   Yes ____   No ____

2. Is the size of the agency important to my career goals?   Yes ____   No ____
     If yes, what size agency am I seeking?

     _____

3. Do I want experiences in a specific specialization?   Yes ____   No ____
     If yes, what specialization?

     _____

4. Am I interested in a specialization with certification requirements?   Yes ____   No ____
     If yes, what specific requirements must be met?

     _____

5. Do I want to work with a specific population (e.g., adults, at risk youth)?   Yes ____   No ____
     If yes, what specific population(s)?

     _____

6. Do I want a site with good post-internship job possibilities?   Yes ____   No ____

7. Should my internship provide opportunities that are *different* from   Yes ____   No ____
     my past experience?

8. Do I need to have a lot of close supervision during my workday?   Yes ____   No ____

List any additional profession-related needs or preferences below:

_____

_____

_____

_____

_____

_____

_____

Personal Needs and Preferences

Not only your profession-related needs and preferences need be taken into account when evaluating an internship site. Your personal situation must also be evaluated to assess whether a given internship site will meet your needs. Chapter One helped you clarify your own personal philosophy, interests and needs. In addition, there are other important personal considerations that must be taken into account in selecting an internship site.

EXERCISE TIME!

The "Personal Needs and Preferences Form" (Figure 3.2) on page 36 gives you some specific questions to answer. Your answers will identify specific personal needs and preferences that may influence your selection of an internship site.

Figure 3.2
Personal Needs and Preferences Form

The following list of questions will help you identify factors to consider when selecting potential internship agencies. Check "yes" or "no" depending upon your own *personal* needs or preferences:

1. Do I need financial or other assistance during my internship?   Yes ___   No ___

    1(a.) Do I need free housing provided by the agency?   Yes ___   No ___

    1(b.) Do I need to have free meals provided by the agency?   Yes ___   No ___

    1(c.) Do I need to receive payment (stipend/salary) for my internship? Yes ___   No ___

2. Will I need convenient transportation arrangements (to/from the agency)?   Yes ___   No ___

3. Do I have significant others that I want to be near during my internship?   Yes ___   No ___
    If so, specify who they are and where they live.

    _____

4. Do I prefer a specific geographic location for my internship?   Yes ___   No ___
    If yes, what specific region, state, or city?

    _____

5. Do I want specific leisure opportunities to be available for me   Yes ___   No ___
at or near my internship site?
    If yes, what specific leisure opportunities?

    _____

6. Do I prefer to spend most of my workday out-of-doors?   Yes ___   No ___

List any additional **personal** *needs or preferences below:*

_____

_____

_____

_____

_____

_____

_____

Search Step #3:
Prioritize Your Needs and Preferences

Now that you have identified your own needs and preferences for your internship, it is important to decide which of these items are the most important to you. To do this, review the two forms (Figures 3.1 and 3.2) you have just completed as part of Step #2. Identify all items receiving a "yes" response, plus those that you have added at the end of each form.

EXERCISE TIME!

After identifying all "yes" responses, plus your additions, on Figures 3.1 and 3.2, use the "Internship Selection Priority Form" (Figure 3.3) on the next page to list the 8 to 10 needs and preferences that are *most* important to your selection of an internship site. Start with the most important item (either profession-related or personal), then list the second most important, and so on. Keep in mind that your internship selection is one of the most important decisions you will make during your academic career. It often determines what direction your professional career takes. Therefore, you should want to place particular emphasis on your *profession-related* needs and preferences.

Figure 3.3
Internship Selection Priority Form

First, list the essential criteria identified in Search Step #1. Then, use the "Profession-related Needs and Preferences Form" and "Personal Needs and Preferences Form" to select your *most* important criterion for an internship site. The most important criterion can be either profession-related or personal, but keep in mind that your internship is important to your professional career. Then list the second most important criterion (either profession-related or personal), and so on.

Essential Criteria

1. Type of agency or organization (include specialization):

    _____

    _____

2. Geographic location (if essential):

    _____

    _____

Needs and Preferences

Priority # 1: _____

_____

Priority # 2: _____

_____

Priority # 3: _____

_____

Priority # 4: _____

_____

Priority # 5: _____

_____

Priority # 6: _____

_____

Priority # 7: _____

_____

Priority # 8: _____

_____

Priority # 9: _____

_____

Priority # 10: _____

_____

Search Step #4:
Identify Resources for Information on Agencies

This section will assist you in identifying many different sources from which to gather internship information. When looking for an internship, *all* sources should be used. Also, remember anyone you speak with could be a lead to the internship position you want. Stay alert, and be ready to market yourself to anyone at any time. You can never be certain where potential leads might come from, or where they may lead.

What are the resources available to you in your area? This is the time to take stock of the resources that will assist you in finding the internship you want. Following are some of the more commonly used and widely available resources which may be of use.

Faculty

Your department's faculty members know a lot about people and agencies providing leisure services. Let your internship coordinator, faculty advisor, and other faculty members know about your professional interests. Ask them to assist with your search for an internship site that meets your needs. It is important, however, not to depend solely on their help. Using *all* of the resources available to you will help you to get the best internship for *you*. Moreover, a thorough search will help when you begin your job search after graduation.

Professionals

Professionals in recreation and leisure are an excellent resource. However, do not wait until you are hunting for an internship to get acquainted. Establish a network early. Come up with a strategy for getting to know specific professionals. For example, you might ask to interview them regarding a specific topic, or regarding opportunities in the field. (Do *not* ask them for an internship or job at this time.) This allows the professional to get to know you before you ask for help with your internship. Professionals usually do not mind giving their assistance if you make specific requests and act in a professional manner.

Placement and Internship Centers

Most colleges and universities have job placement centers which are available to students. Some also have centers that focus exclusively on internships. Become acquainted with these offices and their staff

members early in your college career. Placement and internship offices can offer information in many ways. For example, they provide career placement counseling and testing to those who find it difficult to get started, who feel they are not in tune with themselves and what they have to offer, or who are highly apprehensive about the internship or job search process. They can provide assistance in locating resource directories (see next page), identifying alumni who are employed in leisure services, and writing cover letters and resumes. They may also set up practice interviews, give information on professional grooming skills, and offer other strategies regarding internships and employment.

Resource Directories

Directories are a good way to find out about potential internship agencies. A wide variety of specialized organizations publish directories for distribution to their membership. Generally, these directories give the names and business addresses of members or member organizations, and sometimes they provide details about the agencies listed. A number of leisure-related directories are included among the resources listed in Appendix A.

Libraries

Libraries have many resources. These include reference books, government publications, directories, telephone books, newspapers, magazines, and other pertinent information on internships and employment. If needed, ask the reference librarian for assistance. Although he or she may not be aware of opportunities in leisure services, reference librarians are experts in helping people find the resource they need.

Newspapers

Few internships are advertised in city newspapers; however, closely monitoring classified ads may increase your awareness of leisure services agencies and help you with your job search following graduation. Keep in mind, however, that only 10 percent to 20 percent of potential jobs are listed in the newspaper. Beyond classified ads, city newspapers are excellent resources for learning about new leisure-related businesses in town, identifying key leisure professionals and established businesses, and determining emerging trends and growth patterns. All of these may assist your search for an internship, and later, help identify employment possibilities. Also, most colleges and universities have student-run newspapers, and some of these *do* have classified ads and articles about internships in leisure services. (Tip: It may be helpful to use colored markers to highlight key information in newspapers).

Magazines and Journals

Magazines and journals in recreation and leisure services are often overlooked as resources. Examples of magazines and journals include *Parks and Recreation, Journal of Leisure Research, Journal of Leisurability (Canada), Journal of Parks and Recreation Administration, Therapeutic Recreation Journal, Leisure Sciences, Palaestra,* and *Journal of Physical Education, Recreation and Dance.* Many state Recreation and Park Associations/Societies also publish their own magazines, as do some trade organizations. Although magazines and journals do not generally carry ads for internships, they can help you become aware of opportunities, identify key professionals, and target innovative programs within your specialty. When reviewing any magazine or journal, look at all aspects of the document—articles, advertisements, promotions, etc.

Social Groups (Clubs/Fraternities/Sororities)

Social groups are an instant network of people who share your interests. You may also want to investigate groups in your area which can be of benefit to you, socially and professionally. Share yourself with others and begin to make contacts. Develop your network! An excellent place to start is your school's student-run Recreation and Park Society.

Professional Organizations

Becoming part of a professional organization assists with your professional development. Such organizations include your state's Recreation and Park Society/Association, National Recreation and Park Association, Resort and Commercial Recreation Association, National Therapeutic Recreation Society, American Therapeutic Recreation Association, and the National Association for Interpretation. Leisure-related state and national organizations, with addresses, are provided in Appendices B and C. Involvement in a professional organization indicates your commitment to leisure services, and allows full-time professionals to view your enthusiasm and expertise. Involvement now may not only help you find an internship, but also assist you in finding employment in the field.

Newsletters

A variety of newsletters are published by organizations in leisure services. Most professional organizations have their own newsletter, and these often have information on members and organizational activities. Job listings and internship information are sometimes included in newsletters. Since these newsletters are generally only distributed to members, you should check with your faculty to see what memberships they hold. A wide variety of leisure service agencies also publish their own newsletters, which generally focus upon the activities of their staffs and consumers. Although an agency-specific newsletter may not help you identify a variety of potential internship sites, it will assist you in learning more about a particular agency.

Conferences

Conferences are a good place to network with fellow students and full-time professionals. If obtaining an internship (or employment) is a reason you are attending a conference, be prepared to market yourself. If not, go with the idea of expanding your established network of people. If you have already prepared your resume, be sure to take plenty of copies with you. Whenever you talk with persons who have internship leads, or may serve as resource persons, ask for a business card. When you receive a business card, *do not* just put it away, but turn it over and write some notes about your conversation with the person. This will make it easier to recall the conversation and the individual at a later date. Many conferences also have job marts and resource rooms that provide valuable information on internships and employment in leisure services. For information on upcoming conferences, check with your faculty or contact the professional organizations listed in Appendices B and C.

Friends/Relatives

Take time to convey your aspirations to people close to you. Many times your friends and relatives may not be aware of your chosen career or what you hope to achieve in your professional life. However, these people have your best interest at heart. Also, they are willing to give their time and energy toward your success—but be careful not to overuse your "welcome." You may want to stop here for a moment and consider those friends/relatives you would like to inform of your internship goals.

Internship or Job Announcements

Internship and job announcements (i.e., bulletins, descriptions) are often sent to your faculty by potential supervisors. Also, many professional organizations send internship and job bulletins to members or subscribers (see Appendix A). Check with your faculty to see what bulletins they receive. When reviewing internship and job announcements you should go beyond looking only at the job title, pay, and benefits. Go over the entire announcement carefully. Identify key points. Doing this can give you a clearer idea what the potential internship supervisor or employer is looking for in an applicant, and will give you an edge over other applicants because you are prepared. Also, identify some questions from the announcement you can ask during an interview. Use a magic marker to highlight areas you want to review later. Those areas marked may be formed into interview questions that you could practice before the actual interview.

Employment Agencies

Employment agencies are usually expensive and do not have information on internships. You can do just as good a job of finding an internship (or job) if you follow the recommendations given in this manual. However, employment agencies sometimes do have employment listings which do not show up in other resources.

Telephone Book

When using the phone book make certain you review both the white and yellow pages. If an advertisement in the yellow pages catches your eye, be sure to write down why it caught your eye, and any key words that might be useful to you when you contact the agency or business. If you need information on a specific geographical area, you can usually find telephone books in your university or public library. You can also buy a telephone book for that area from the telephone company, if you prefer.

Networking

Networking is the key to your search for an internship and, later, employment. Your networking strategy should have the same effect as dropping a stone in water. When the stone hits the water, a rippling (i.e., rings) effect takes place with the ripples expanding wider and wider. That is what your network should be. Every person you meet is a contact and a potential lead. Learning how to develop and nurture a professional network will benefit you throughout your professional career.

The "Contact Record Sheets" (Figure 3.4) on the following pages provide a system to track your internship contacts. This chart is simple to use and keeps key people within reach for continuous contact. You may want to copy the Contact Record Sheet to record additional contacts. The Contact Record Sheet is a quick and easy reference guide.

Figure 3.4 Contact Record Sheet

1.

Contact Person

Company name

Street

City

State   Zip   Phone Number

Comments

Information requested _____

Phone log _____

DATE

Cover letter/Resume submitted _____

2.

Contact Person

Company name

Street

City

State   Zip   Phone Number

Comments

Information requested _____

Phone log _____

DATE

Cover letter/Resume submitted _____

3.

Contact Person

Company name

Street

City

State   Zip   Phone Number

Comments

Information requested _____

Phone log _____

DATE

Cover letter/Resume submitted _____

Figure 3.4 Contact Record Sheet (continued)

4.

Contact Person

Company name

Street

City

State   Zip   Phone Number

Comments

Information requested _____

_____

Phone log _____

_____
_____
_____
_____
_____

DATE

Cover letter/Resume submitted _____

5.

Contact Person

Company name

Street

City

State   Zip   Phone Number

Comments

Information requested _____

_____

Phone log _____

_____
_____
_____
_____
_____

DATE

Cover letter/Resume submitted _____

6.

Contact Person

Company name

Street

City

State   Zip   Phone Number

Comments

Information requested _____

_____

Phone log _____

_____
_____
_____
_____

DATE

Cover letter/Resume submitted _____

Search Step #5:
Compile a List of Potential Internship Agencies

Now that you have completed the above tasks, it is time to begin your search for *specific* agencies or organizations that meet your essential criteria (Step #1) *and* offer as many of your prioritized needs and preferences as possible (Step #3). Using your resources (Step #4), identify internship sites that meet your essential criteria; then, compare your prioritized needs and preferences with what each site offers. Compile a list of agencies that appear to offer you what you are looking for in an internship agency.

Be selective. Don't try to list *every* agency or organization. If an agency appears to be a good prospect for you because it meets the most important items on your prioritized list, include it. Your final list of potential internship agencies should include five to eight agencies that are the best "fit" with your prioritized needs and preferences. Once you have this list, you are well on you way to finding your "ideal" internship site.

RESEARCH

Once you have identified your priorities and reduced your list of potential internship agencies to a manageable number, it is time to begin an *intensive* research process. This process is intended to give you as much information as possible about your potential agencies *before* making formal application for an internship. How do you get this information? You may need to read agency brochures or reports, job descriptions/announcements, financial statements, visit the organization, and talk with people who work at the agency.

Start the research process with the agency that appears to offer you the best possible internship, but don't confine your research to a single agency. You should gather detailed information on at least three to five of your preferred agencies.

Your research is crucial—it enables you to get the information you need to select your internship site. It also allows you to show the "best you" to potential internship supervisors. Internship supervisors are looking for well-prepared students who can sell themselves and their abilities. Gaining information about a potential internship agency before an interview will give you an edge in your quest for the best possible internship.

University Files and Resources

Some universities maintain extensive files on prospective internship agencies. These files often contain detailed information on an agency, such as annual reports, newsletters, promotional materials, or agency descriptions written by previous interns. Check with your internship coordinator or university internship office to see if files exist for the agencies on your list. If so, make sure that the materials are thorough and up-to-date. If no files exist or the materials are out-of-date, you will have to make direct contact with the agency to gather the information you need.

Telephone Calls

The telephone is useful in gaining information about an agency and determining to whom your cover letter and resume should be sent. A phone call also may reveal that an agency is not accepting interns; thus, allowing you to concentrate your efforts on other agencies. Be assertive, but not aggressive in your preliminary informational telephone calls. Also, by asking for exactly what you want (e.g., promotional brochures, newsletters, annual reports, name of recreation director), you are more likely to be helped. You may have to call more than once to get the name of the person or the information you need. Be ready to sell yourself in the

event you are transferred directly to a potential internship supervisor. He or she may want to conduct an internship interview right on the spot; however, it is better to explain that you are still researching agencies and would prefer to set up a formal interview at a later date. Unless you are *certain* that this agency is ideal for you, it is important not to make commitments during your research process.

Mail

The mail is an effective tool, if used properly. A well-written request letter allows you to make a good first impression and enables you to specify exactly what information you want. Remember, a specific request is harder to ignore than a vague one. Directing mail to a specific individual is recommended, but be *certain* that you know the person's correct title and correct spelling of his or her name. Do not just mail your request and wait indefinitely. After a pre-planned period of time, two to three weeks, make a follow-up telephone call. Check to make sure the agency received your request for information. If the information has not yet been sent, ask when you might expect to receive it.

Visit Site

If possible, visit the site before your interview to better prepare yourself. By making a visitation you will: (1) know how to get there and how long it will take; (2) be aware of the atmosphere of the company—formal or informal; (3) perhaps run into someone you know who could put in a good word for you; (4) meet the receptionist and establish rapport early; and (5) obtain additional information for your use. Also, an informational site visit may reveal that this agency really isn't what you are looking for in an internship site.

Making a Pre-interview Appointment

If you are seeking employment at an internship site, you may want to make a pre-interview appointment with the person who will be conducting interviews. This will help clarify any information you may need for the upcoming interview. If a pre-interview appointment is not possible, but you are able to speak with the receptionist, ask his or her name and then ask for him or her by name when you arrive for your interview. People like to be called by name, but be sure not to be too informal.

Contacts Within Agency

If you know anyone familiar with the agency, talk to him or her about the company's philosophy, goals, future plans, etc. The better you know the company, the better you will do in an interview and the better the chance that you will select the internship site that is "right" for you.

Speak with Current or Past Interns at the Agency

If you know current or past interns at the agency, talk to them for another perspective on the agency. This information will help to ensure that the agency can meet your professional goals. It may also assist you in your interview and increase your knowledge of specific jobs available to interns. Be prepared with questions, and thank them for their assistance.

Volunteer at the Agency

Many recreation and leisure agencies need volunteer help to support their programs and activities. Volunteering for at least one program will enable you to get to know the agency and its services "first hand." Volunteering is time consuming, but it is worth it. It not only provides you with information, but it allows you to demonstrate your knowledge and skills to important agency personnel. Volunteering also adds to your resume, even if you decide against applying for an internship at that agency.

SUMMARY

This chapter provided a systematic process for identifying potential internship agencies and narrowing your selections to a manageable number of sites. Learning how to search for an internship site, including identification of resources and "Networking," is a necessary strategy. Effective networking is especially valuable, now and in the future. You should continue to network throughout your career.

This chapter also identified ways to research information you need to consider in your internship selection process. Becoming familiar with an agency before you make contact, and especially before your internship interview, can give you an edge. Sometimes your research reveals that this isn't the agency for you, but it also can confirm that this is your "ideal" agency.

Now it is time to combine the chapters that you have completed and to develop the tools that will market your talents and abilities. The next two chapters will assist you in developing essential internship tools, or aid in the refinement of tools you already have. Remember, completing the preceding chapters is vital for developing high-quality internship tools.

CHAPTER FOUR

Preparation: The Cover Letter

"We cannot direct the wind . . . but we can adjust the sails."
—Napoleon Hill

It is very easy to turn directly to this chapter, skipping the others, in your haste to get started in your internship preparation. If you have done so, you have missed the chapters that can give you the edge over other applicants. This chapter is important because the end result is your first formal communication with the prospective internship supervisor—your cover letter. However, what leads up to this point is vital to your success. If you have not read Chapter One through Chapter Three (and completed the exercises they contain), you should return to the beginning of the manual and start from there.

To develop your ***cover letter***, you need to:

• Understand acceptable formats for a cover letter,

• Know the appropriate content of a cover letter, and

• Review examples of cover letters.

THE COVER LETTER

The cover letter is the letter you write to potential internship sites to inform them of your interest and to let them know that your resume is enclosed for their review. It is more than a formality—it is crucial. The cover letter is often the first thing the potential internship supervisor sees and, in some cases, it is more valuable than the resume. The importance of making a good first impression cannot be overemphasized. The cover letter offers a chance for you to let a potential internship supervisor know that you are truly excited about his or her agency and the prospect of learning from him or her. The cover letter also gives you the opportunity to demonstrate that you have an *essential* skill, the ability to communicate clearly and effectively in writing. Moreover, the cover letter provides a chance to emphasize aspects of your resume that may be particularly important to the agency receiving your letter. When a potential internship supervisor reads your cover letter, you want him or her to know that you are enthusiastic, bright, energetic, and qualified.

Format of a Cover Letter

Since the cover letter is so important, it is your task to create a cover letter which looks professional and catches the potential internship supervisor's eye. Even before beginning to read your cover letter, a potential internship supervisor will have begun to form an impression of you. The appearance of your cover letter and mailing envelope will let him or her know if you are the type of student who takes pride in your written work, attends to important details, and understands how to correspond in a professional manner. A well-constructed cover letter is your initial step toward making a good first impression.

Cover letters should be original and, if possible, confined to one page. Black type on quality white paper (20# bond with at least 25 percent cotton content) is still the accepted standard, preferably done on a computer and printed on a laser printer. Dot matrix printers should be avoided unless absolutely necessary. Remember that mass-produced cover letters and random mailings of internship materials are rarely productive.

The primary considerations in formatting your cover letter are balance and consistency. These two factors, combined with a conventional formal letter writing lay-out, result in a cover letter that has "eye appeal" and encourages the recipient to start reading. All cover letters should correspond to the following points:

(1) The amount of white space on the letter is about the same on the top and bottom—the right and left sides are about equal, too.

(2) An extra space is used *between* entries (date and address, paragraphs, etc.); otherwise, single spacing is used.

(3) The contact person's full name, title, agency, and address are given.

(4) Except in unusual circumstances, the person's formal name (e.g., Mr., Dr., Ms. with his/her last name only) is used, followed by a *colon.*

(5) Three extra spaces are left blank between "Sincerely," and the writer's typed name. The writer's signature (black ink is preferred) goes in the middle of this space.

(6) The name, *present* address and phone (optional) of the writer are given.

(7) Use of "Enclosure" lets the reader know that something else is enclosed; in this case, the resume. Using the abbreviation "Enc." is also acceptable.

Four slightly different formats of the same cover letter are shown in the following four pages (Figures 4.1 through 4.4). These are the most widely accepted formats for cover letters, and we have added comments to help you identify the unique features of each format. Which one you select is a matter of personal preference; however, no matter which format you prefer, be sure to pay close attention to details (e.g., margin alignment, spacing). Note that each of these letters conforms to all seven of the above points. A completed cover letter must be carefully examined to be sure it conforms to an accepted format and to *all* points listed above.

Figure 4.1
Cover Letter—*Block Format*

Date of Typing ——————— | Date is placed at left margin. |

Mr. William Brown
Director of Recreation
Parkendale Recreation and Parks Department
1011 Duke Drive
Parkendale, CA 95465 | First word in each paragraph is *not* indented. |

Dear Mr. Brown:

I read with interest your article entitled, "Creative Financing." I have studied this subject in my courses at West Coast State University, and am currently looking for an internship site that will enhance my understanding of public recreation and creative financing methods.

During my college career, I have had the pleasure to work with many community agencies on various fund raising projects. These experiences have given me the ability to create, develop, and sell ideas and products. Also, I have been elected Northern California Student Representative to the California Park and Recreation Society, Student Branch, and Vice President of the Recreation Student Association at West Coast State University.

Our university's 12-week internship offers me an exciting opportunity to learn from progressive public recreation professionals. Glenda Thomas, a past intern with your agency, indicated that you and your staff could offer me exactly the type of experience I am seeking. Moreover, your promotional brochures and last year's annual report make it clear that the Parkendale Recreation and Parks Department offers innovative programs that are based upon sound management principles. I know that I could learn a great deal from an internship with your agency.

I would like to meet you to further discuss the possibility of our working together. I will call you during the week of April 12th to discuss the possibility of an interview. Thank you for your time and efforts on my behalf.

Sincerely,

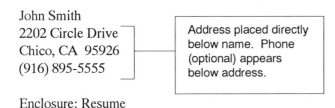

John Smith
2202 Circle Drive
Chico, CA 95926
(916) 895-5555 | Address placed directly below name. Phone (optional) appears below address. |

Enclosure: Resume

Figure 4.2
Cover Letter—*Block Format (Alternate)*

Address and phone (optional) at top and indented about 2/3rds across page for balance. **Note**: Name is not given here.

2202 Circle Drive
Chico, CA 95926
(916) 895-5555

Date of Typing

Mr. William Brown
Director of Recreation
Parkendale Recreation and Parks Department
1011 Duke Drive
Parkendale, CA 95465

Rest of letter conforms to same block format as Figure 4-1.

Dear Mr. Brown:

I read with interest your article entitled, "Creative Financing." I have studied this subject in my courses at West Coast State University, and am currently looking for an internship site that will enhance my understanding of public recreation and creative financing methods.

During my college career, I have had the pleasure to work with many community agencies on various fund raising projects. These experiences have given me the ability to create, develop, and sell ideas and products. Also, I have been elected Northern California Student Representative to the California Park and Recreation Society, Student Branch, and Vice President of the Recreation Student Association at West Coast State University.

Our university's 12-week internship offers me an exciting opportunity to learn from progressive public recreation professionals. Glenda Thomas, a past intern with your agency, indicated that you and your staff could offer me exactly the type of experience I am seeking. Moreover, your promotional brochures and last year's annual report make it clear that the Parkendale Recreation and Parks Department offers innovative programs that are based upon sound management principles. I know that I could learn a great deal from an internship with your agency.

I would like to meet you to further discuss the possibility of our working together. I will call you during the week of April 12th to discuss the possibility of an interview. Thank you for your time and efforts on my behalf.

Sincerely,

John Smith

Enclosure: Resume

Figure 4.3
Cover Letter—*Modified Block Format*

Date indented about 2/3rds across page. ———— Date of Typing

Mr. William Brown
Director of Recreation
Parkendale Recreation and Parks Department
1011 Duke Drive
Parkendale, CA 95465

First word in each paragraph indented five spaces.

Dear Mr. Brown:

     I read with interest your article entitled, "Creative Financing." I have studied this subject in my courses at West Coast State University, and am currently looking for an internship site that will enhance my understanding of public recreation and creative financing methods.

     During my college career, I have had the pleasure to work with many community agencies on various fund raising projects. These experiences have given me the ability to create, develop, and sell ideas and products. Also, I have been elected Northern California Student Representative to the California Park and Recreation Society, Student Branch, and Vice President of the Recreation Student Association at West Coast State University.

     Our university's 12-week internship offers me an exciting opportunity to learn from progressive public recreation professionals. Glenda Thomas, a past intern with your agency, indicated that you and your staff could offer me the exactly the type of experience I am seeking. Moreover, your promotional brochures and last year's annual report make it clear that the Parkendale Recreation and Parks Department offers innovative programs that are based upon sound management principles. I know that I could learn a great deal from an internship with your agency.

     I would like to meet you to further discuss the possibility of our working together. I will call you during the week of April 12th to discuss the possibility of an interview. Thank you for your time and efforts on my behalf.

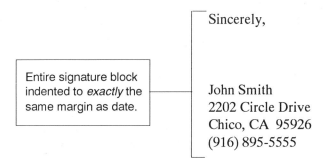

Sincerely,

Entire signature block indented to *exactly* the same margin as date.

John Smith
2202 Circle Drive
Chico, CA 95926
(916) 895-5555

Enclosure: Resume

Figure 4.4
Cover Letter—*Modified Block Format (Alternate)*

Address and phone (optional) placed on same margin and one space above date.

2202 Circle Drive
Chico, CA 95926
(916) 895-5555

Date of Typing

Mr. William Brown
Director of Recreation
Parkendale Recreation and Parks Department
1011 Duke Drive
Parkendale, CA 95465

Rest of letter conforms to same modified block format as Figure 4-3.

Dear Mr. Brown:

I read with interest your article entitled, "Creative Financing." I have studied this subject in my courses at West Coast State University, and am currently looking for an internship site that will enhance my understanding of public recreation and creative financing methods.

During my college career, I have had the pleasure to work with many community agencies on various fund raising projects. These experiences have given me the ability to create, develop, and sell ideas and products. Also, I have been elected Northern California Student Representative to the California Park and Recreation Society, Student Branch, and Vice President of the Recreation Student Association at West Coast State University.

Our university's 12-week internship offers me an exciting opportunity to learn from progressive public recreation professionals. Glenda Thomas, a past intern with your agency, indicated that you and your staff could offer me the exactly the type of experience I am seeking. Moreover, your promotional brochures and last year's annual report make it clear that the Parkendale Recreation and Parks Department offers innovative programs that are based upon sound management principles. I know that I could learn a great deal from an internship with your agency.

I would like to meet you to further discuss the possibility of our working together. I will call you during the week of April 12th to discuss the possibility of an interview. Thank you for your time and efforts on my behalf.

Sincerely,

John Smith

Enclosure: Resume

Content of Cover Letter

The body of a cover letter has four important parts, which are often addressed in separate paragraphs. The four parts of a well-prepared cover letter are:

(1) *Introduction.* The first paragraph should let the potential internship supervisor know why you are writing to him or her. This paragraph gives some information, but its primary function is to create a favorable impression, and to let the potential supervisor know that you are interested in an internship with his or her agency. Avoid generic openings such as: "I'm a senior in college", or "I would like to apply for an internship . . .". An effective beginning may be to refer to individuals who recommended the agency (e.g., faculty members, professionals), or explain how you found out about the opportunities offered at the agency (e.g., newspaper advertisements, notices in journals). Referring to such information shows the employer you have taken the time to gather your facts. This paragraph should also indicate that you are interested in the *possibility* of doing an internship with the agency.

Note: Because some professionals are not familiar with the term "internship," you may want to use other terms in addition to "internship" such as on-the-job training, apprenticeship, co-op, or management trainee.

(2) *Connection.* This paragraph of the cover letter describes to the prospective internship supervisor your knowledge of the agency, and how your skills and career interests "match" the agency's needs. Briefly summarize *important* aspects of your resume, plus any other information that may not appear in the resume (e.g., specific courses you have taken). The main purpose of the connection paragraph is to convince the prospective supervisor that you have skills that will benefit the agency during your internship.

(3) *Personalization.* You not only want a prospective internship supervisor to know you are qualified to be an intern, but you also want him or her to know you hope to learn a great deal from your internship experience. The third paragraph allows you to personalize; thus, you let the potential supervisor know what it is about the agency that is important to you. What are they doing that you want to be a part of? What unique learning experiences do they offer? This information can only be obtained by researching the company (see Chapter Three).

Note: Many students and professionals prefer to combine the Connection and Personalization aspects into a single paragraph. Some examples of three-paragraph cover letters are included in this chapter.

(4) *Closing.* The final paragraph answers the question, What happens next?" You need to let the prospective internship supervisor know that you plan to follow-up by phone to discuss the possibility of doing an internship with his or her agency. Do *not* wait to be contacted by the agency! Also let him or her know that you would appreciate a personal interview. Do not demand an interview—the prospective supervisor should control future meetings. If the distance is too great for you to visit the agency, request a telephone interview. Finally, you should express your appreciation to the prospective supervisor.

With a cover letter (and resume, too), it's not only *what* you say, but *how* you say it that counts. Potential internship supervisors are looking for students who attend to details and avoid errors in their work. You can demonstrate this in your cover letter by using correct grammar and avoiding spelling and typographical errors. In general, you should also avoid using abbreviations, acronyms, and contractions. In order to send the best possible cover letter, we urge you to type *individually* each letter using a computer with laser printer and:

- put the completed letter aside for at least 24 hours, then carefully reread it at least four times;

- when you think it is perfect, give it to a *knowledgeable* friend or relative to read for comprehension, grammar and spelling; and,

- *always* use a computer spell checking program prior to final printing of your cover letter do not depend exclusively upon this, however. (See Box "When a Computerized Spell Check Fails" see page 57.)

When a Computerized Spell Check Fails

Computer spell checking software programs are essential to use, but they cannot take the place of careful proofreading. Spell checkers only identify words that are misspelled; therefore, they do not identify the *wrong* word that is spelled correctly. The following humorous mistakes were actually submitted by students. They may have used spell checkers, but they did *not* proofread:

"My work as a camp counselor has helped me gain valuable experience in ants and crafts."

"While working at my present job, I have served as a leader for sex groups of adults."

"I also have sigh language skills."

"I enjoy being in the presents of other people."

"This exorcise helped me to understand how to work better with others."

"I have worked hard to create a homely environment for participants."

"My day damp experiences have helped me to understand the needs of children."

"I have used my sign language skills to serve as an interrupter for a person who is deaf."

"My research indicates that your resort plans to add 800 hotel tooms to its thriving business." (Note: A spell checker *would* have caught this one)

Final Tips and Reminders About the Cover Letter

(1) Try to mail your cover letter and resume so it arrives during the middle of the week. Mondays usually bring a lot of mail and Fridays are often hectic.

(2) Be sure to address your letter to a specific person, and include his or her job title. Double check your spelling of the person's name prior to mailing.

(3) Follow-up by phone within one week of the letter's arrival to discuss the possibility of an interview.

(4) Use high-quality paper that is identical to your resume. We suggest 20# bond with at least 25 percent cotton content.

(5) Use a high-quality envelope to mail your cover letter and resume, and make sure that it is addressed properly (typed and free from spelling errors). If possible, have the envelope match the paper you are using for the cover letter and resume. Remember, a good first impression is vital, and the first thing a potential internship supervisor sees is your envelope.

EXERCISE TIME!

The cover letter on the next page (Figure 4.5) is intended to help you identify errors in both format and content in a cover letter. At this point, test your understanding of cover letters by circling the errors and missing information in Figure 4.5; then, turn to page 61 (Figure 4.6) for the answers.

September 2, 1991

Ms. Anna E. Bell
Mapac, Inc.
1205 Baker Street, Suite 120
San Francisco, CA 94001

Dear Anna Bell,

Since our discussion on August 19th, I have had the oppurtunity to meet with Dr. Joseph Bright, my internship coordinator. He agreed with me that completing an internship with Mapac in the Department of Public Relations would be an excellent learning experience. I look forward to the possibility of contributing my creativity and knowledge of public relations to your organization.

Currently, I am finishing my capstone courses at West Coast State University in both my business and communication majors. I am especially excited about my business law and international communication classes. Both of these courses are teaching me practical skills that will help me contribute to your department and assist me in my professional growth.

I will be in San Francisco on September 27th, and would appreciate it if we could get together to discuss my doing an internship with Mapac. I will call you during the week of September 16th to establish a time for our meeting.

Sincerely,

Sally Doe
1111 Cherry Street
Chico, CA 95926
(916) 891-2222

Figure 4.6
(Answers to Figure 4.5)

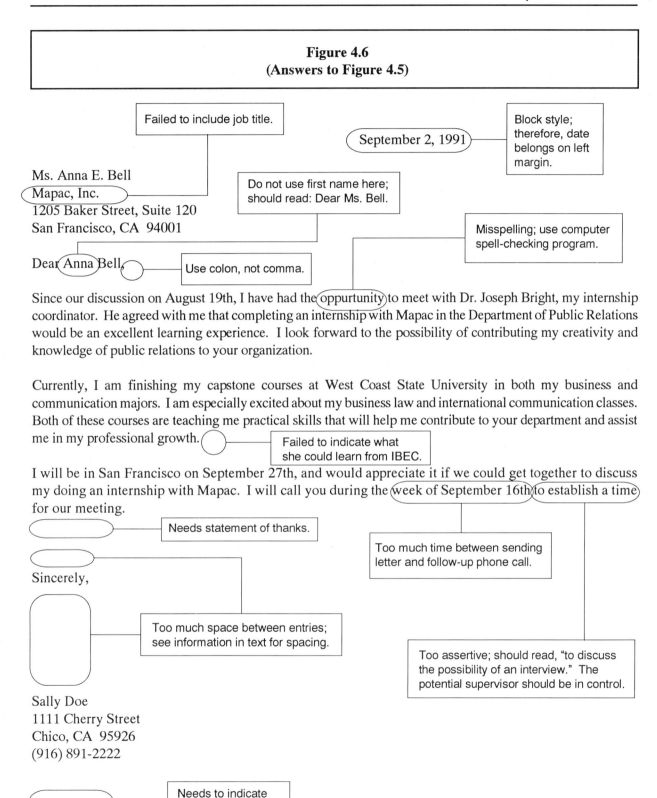

Failed to include job title.

September 2, 1991

Block style; therefore, date belongs on left margin.

Ms. Anna E. Bell
Mapac, Inc.
1205 Baker Street, Suite 120
San Francisco, CA 94001

Do not use first name here; should read: Dear Ms. Bell.

Misspelling; use computer spell-checking program.

Dear Anna Bell,

Use colon, not comma.

Since our discussion on August 19th, I have had the oppurtunity to meet with Dr. Joseph Bright, my internship coordinator. He agreed with me that completing an internship with Mapac in the Department of Public Relations would be an excellent learning experience. I look forward to the possibility of contributing my creativity and knowledge of public relations to your organization.

Currently, I am finishing my capstone courses at West Coast State University in both my business and communication majors. I am especially excited about my business law and international communication classes. Both of these courses are teaching me practical skills that will help me contribute to your department and assist me in my professional growth.

Failed to indicate what she could learn from IBEC.

I will be in San Francisco on September 27th, and would appreciate it if we could get together to discuss my doing an internship with Mapac. I will call you during the week of September 16th to establish a time for our meeting.

Needs statement of thanks.

Too much time between sending letter and follow-up phone call.

Sincerely,

Too much space between entries; see information in text for spacing.

Too assertive; should read, "to discuss the possibility of an interview." The potential supervisor should be in control.

Sally Doe
1111 Cherry Street
Chico, CA 95926
(916) 891-2222

Needs to indicate resume is enclosed.

Cover Letter Examples

Carefully review the cover letters provided on the next six pages. They are good examples of letters that may help you. Use them for guidance, but be sure to write *your* letter in your own style and wording. Note that some of these letters may deviate slightly from the content guidelines given above. It is not essential that your letters conform *exactly* to our content guidelines, but it is important that all necessary information is included in a neat, well-formatted, and error-free cover letter.

Sample Cover Letter #1

Date of Typing

Ms. Anna E. Bell
Director of Public Relations
Mapac, Inc.
1205 Baker Street, Suite 120
San Francisco, CA 94001

Dear Ms. Bell:

Since our discussion on (date), I have had the opportunity to meet with Dr. Joseph Bright, my internship coordinator. He agreed with me that completing an internship with Mapac in the Department of Public Relations would be an excellent learning experience. I look forward to the possibility of contributing my creativity and knowledge of public relations to your organization.

Currently, I am finishing my capstone courses at West Coast State University in both my business and communication majors. I am especially enthusiastic about my business law and international communication classes. Both of these courses are teaching me practical skills that will help me contribute to your department and assist me in my professional growth.

Working with your department would give me an understanding of the requirements of an entry level position at Mapac. In addition, it would offer me the opportunity to work with knowledgeable professionals, and to integrate classroom theory and practical experience. I am very excited about the possibility of working with you.

I will be in San Francisco on (date), and would appreciate it if we could get together to discuss my doing an internship with Mapac. I will call you during the week of (date) to discuss the possibility of an interview. Thank you for your interest and your time.

Sincerely,

Sally Doe
1111 Cherry Street
Chico, CA 95926
(916) 891-2222

Enclosure: Resume

Sample Cover Letter #2

Date of Typing

Mr. Thomas Black
Personnel Department
Enjoyable Hotel and Resort
P.O. Box 2000
Palmero, CA 98201

Dear Mr. Black:

Dr. Denise Smart, my academic advisor, suggested I contact you with regard to doing an internship in conjunction with your management training program. Your resort was highly recommended by Dr. Smart, who considers Enjoyable one of the leaders in the hotel industry.

Upon completion of my internship in June, I will receive my Bachelor of Science Degree in Recreation and Hospitality Management at Southwest University. Currently, I am working for the Vacation Inn in Bordertown, NM, assisting with development of training programs for minority employees. I am fluent in Spanish and a native Southern Californian, and I find these strengths to be an asset in the hotel industry. I am also a working member of the American Hotel Association.

I would like to be a part of Enjoyable Hotel and Resort's growth. Your quality organization and training program would provide me with a unique opportunity to advance my skills. At the same time, my strong background in organization of people and customer service would enable me to make a significant contribution to your company. My resume is enclosed for your review. I know your company has a lot to offer an intern, and I feel I can also be an asset to Enjoyable Hotel and Resort.

Thank you for your time. I will call within ten days to discuss this request with you. If Enjoyable has a formal application for its management training program, please send it to me and I will complete it and return it promptly.

Sincerely,

John Smith
2000 Circle Drive
Bordertown, NM 84260
(505) 895-5555

Enc.: Resume

Sample Cover Letter #3

700 West Main Street
University City, PA 16756

Date of Typing

Mr. Robert Saunders
Manager/Owner
Fitness For Life
400 Martin Ave.
University City, PA 16755

Dear Mr. Saunders:

After many years of athletic involvement through competitive swimming and running, I am eager to start my career in the fitness industry. Through my university's career file, I have learned that your agency has previously accepted Northeast State University students for their internship (Practicum) experiences. Please consider me a candidate for an internship with your organization during the coming fall semester.

I have been a member of your club since (date of membership), and have a general understanding of the facility and its operations. My athletic experience has given me the opportunity to visit and utilize a variety of facilities, and I have worked with people of all ages and physical abilities. Through my Practicum, I would like to learn more about your agency's operation, especially the areas of marketing and advertising. Northeast's Practicum experience is twelve weeks in length and forty hours per week. I believe that Fitness For Life can add to my college experience and give me a better understanding of the industry I am preparing to enter.

I would appreciate the opportunity to discuss my Practicum with you in further detail. I will call you at your office the week of (specify week), to discuss the possibly of an interview. Thank you for your time.

Sincerely,

Annie J. Jones

Enclosure

Sample Cover Letter #4

750 Devonshire Drive
Warmsville, FL 11447
(407) 238-7513

Date of Typing

Mr. Brian Fitzpatrick
Chief Ranger
Fantasy Island National Seashore
Route 24, Box 111
Burlington, MD 21722

Dear Mr. Fitzpatrick:

My sister was an intern at Fantasy Island National Seashore during the summer of (year). As a result, I know that you have an excellent program that offers interns a wide variety of learning experiences. I am extremely interested in being a part of your organization as an intern this summer.

I have had two summers of experience working in national parks, plus numerous park-related academic courses. Also, I have specialized training in CPR and Advanced First Aid, and am qualified as a National Forest Firefighter. As a student majoring in Recreation and Parks at Dolphin College, I am interested in gaining experience in park management, particularly visitor management. I am eager to learn from you and your staff, and feel that the experience I have gained while in college will make me an asset to your department.

I would appreciate an opportunity to discuss my qualifications and the possibility of doing an internship at Fantasy Island. I will contact you during the week of (date) to discuss the possibility of an interview. Thank you for your time.

Sincerely,

Penny D. Gonglewski

Enclosure: Resume

Sample Cover Letter #5

Date of Typing

Ms. Mary Sue Wilson
Director of Therapeutic Recreation
Williamstown Hospital
328 Jefferson Highway
Williamstown, MO 58391

Dear Ms. Wilson:

I recently read about your innovative Therapeutic Recreation program, and am excited about the learning opportunities it could offer me. Beginning in January, I will participate in a twelve-week internship in Therapeutic Recreation as part of my study at Showmee University. Physical rehabilitation is my emphasis; therefore, your program corresponds with my professional interests.

During the past two years, I have worked as a Physical Therapy Assistant at St. Helen's Hospital. This experience has helped prepare me for working with individuals who required specialized therapeutic procedures. In addition, I have designed activity and exercise programs for a variety of groups.

I strongly believe that a dynamic internship experience is essential to one's education. It enables an individual to put classroom theory into practical application. An academic internship at Williamstown Hospital would be an exciting opportunity, and would provide the learning experience I am seeking.

I would appreciate meeting with you to outline my experiences as well as my internship goals. I will call your office during the week of (date) to discuss the possibility of an interview. Thank you for your time and consideration.

Sincerely,

Holly T. Farr
724 Worthington Road
Lester, MO 47750

Enclosure

Sample Cover Letter #6

433 East Badger Avenue
Nessle, NC 30975

Date of Typing

Mr. Larry LaMont
Head Golf Professional
Elite Country Club
300 Commerce Drive
Pleasantville, NC 19000

Dear Mr. LaMont:

After planning and coordinating a celebrity golf tournament to benefit disadvantaged youth at your country club, I became interested in the possibility of doing my co-op (internship) under your supervision. The efficiency of your operation and the professional behavior of your entire staff convinced me that I could learn a great deal from working at Elite.

My course of study at Fairway State has provided me with knowledge in a variety of important areas, including turf management, marketing, and retail operations. In addition, my courses in leisure studies have aided my understanding of human behavior and helped prepare me for teaching golf to persons with varying skill levels. I believe my academic preparation, combined with my golfing skills (2 handicap), would enable me to make a significant contribution to your program. I also feel that the professionalism exemplified by your golf operation would provide me with the proper learning environment to advance in the golf industry.

I would like to meet with you to discuss my qualifications and the possibility of completing a twelve-week co-operative at Elite Country Club. I will call your office the week of (date) to see about setting up an interview.

Sincerely,

Perry Schlow-Backswing

Enclosure

SUMMARY

This chapter has provided information, exercises and examples for writing your cover letter. It emphasized the importance of a well prepared cover letter, including attention to both content and format. The cover letter does not stand alone, however. It introduces you to a prospective internship supervisor and highlights your resume, which accompanies the cover letter. Together, a quality cover letter and resume will increase your chances of getting the internship you desire

Now it is time to begin preparing your resume. The next chapter will provide you with information on creating a professional resume that attracts and holds the attention of a potential internship supervisor. Like Chapter Four, the next chapter will also provide exercises and examples to help you. The end result will be a resume you can distribute with pride.

CHAPTER FIVE

Preparation: The Resume

"Nothing which has entered into our experience is ever lost"
—William Ellery Channing

No written document is more important to your internship plans than your resume, and few documents take more time and effort to prepare. This chapter will help you develop your profesional resume, with special attention to the "little" things that will make your resume stand out. This chapter will also provide you with examples of resumes that have proven effective in securing internships in recreation and leisure services.

To Construct the best possible resume, you need to:

- Develop a "foundation" or "working" resume,

- Know what a "professional resume" is, including acceptable formats and appropriate content, and

- Review examples of resumes.

THE RESUME

Your resume is more than a written summary of your experiences, skills, achievements, and interests—it is your own personal marketing device. It provides you with an opportunity to "sell" yourself to a potential internship agency and, like the cover letter, it offers a chance to demonstrate your professional writing skills to a potential internship supervisor. A well-organized, attractive, and informative resume not only helps you secure the best possible internship, but it will prove invaluable when you prepare your employment resume prior to graduation.

Will a good resume get you the internship you seek? Probably not, but a bad one certainly can *lose* it for you! A poorly constructed, inconsistent, or error-filled resume may result in your being eliminated from consideration without an interview. A properly prepared resume, however, will attract the reader's attention and go a long way toward securing the interview you need.

Unfortunately, there is no magical formula for preparing the "perfect" resume. Each potential internship supervisor has his or her own personal preferences regarding the format and content of a resume. Nevertheless, there are a lot of things you can do to ensure that your resume is complete and appeals to the maximum number of professionals in recreation and leisure services. The information in this chapter is based upon a wide variety of written sources, plus many conversations with internship supervisors. It is intended to help you prepare the best possible resume—a resume that will open the interview doors for the internship that *you* want.

The "Foundation" or "Working" Resume

To build your resume, we suggest you create two documents containing information for your use. First, construct what we call a "foundation" (or "working") resume. This document will contain everything there is to know about you. Just write down everything that you think might be important; i.e., all education, work experiences (paid/volunteer), achievements, certificates, workshops and seminars attended, hobbies/recreational pursuits, hospitalizations and potential references. Don't worry about the format. Just put information down. Some of this information may seem irrelevant; however, experience teaches us there may be times when you will use this information. It is always better to be prepared.

EXERCISE TIME!

To help you, we have included a Foundation Resume Worksheet (Figure 5.1; pages 73 to 75) in this chapter. Use this worksheet to list *all* information about yourself that *might* be useful to a prospective internship supervisor. Later, you can use this foundation resume to pick and choose any combination of information or facts which meet the criteria for the specific internship (or employment) position you are seeking. After you select the information you need, you can begin to polish the content in preparation for your "professional" resume.

Figure 5.1
Foundation Resume Worksheet

Name, Address, Phone (Local and Permanent) _____

_____

_____

_____

_____

Career Objective (Optional) _____

_____

_____

_____

Skills/Accomplishments _____

_____

_____

_____

_____

Education _____

_____

_____

_____

_____

_____

_____

Figure 5.1
Foundation Resume Worksheet (continued)

Workshops/Seminars Attended _____

_____

_____

_____

_____

_____

_____

Work (Business) Experience _____

_____

_____

_____

_____

_____

_____

_____

_____

Awards, Honors, and Certificates _____

_____

_____

_____

_____

_____

Figure 5.1
Foundation Resume Worksheet (continued)

Memberships _____

_____

_____

_____

_____

References (Include Addresses/Phones) _____

_____

_____

_____

_____

Medical History _____

_____

_____

_____

Interest and Hobbies _____

_____

_____

_____

Other Pertinent Information

_____

_____

_____

The "Professional" Resume

The second document is the typical resume used by professionals—the one that most people think of when they hear the word "resume." It is the one- or two-page resume that you will use the majority of the time. A two-page resume is preferred by most recreation and leisure professionals; however, employers for large, commercial businesses recommend keeping your resume to one page. The amount of experience you have may also dictate the length of your resume.

Most experts suggest using either a *chronological* resume, which lists specific experiences in order by dates, or a *functional* resume, which documents skills, knowledge, abilities and accomplishments, without emphasizing dates. Generally, the functional resume is better for the person who has been out of the job market for an extended period of time, or has gaps between experiences that are difficult to explain.

Generally, students and professionals in recreation and leisure services prefer to use the chronological resume. Therefore, this chapter will focus on the chronological resume. We do, however, suggest you consider adding a section to your chronological resume that lists specific skills. If you believe a functional resume is best for you, we suggest you consult the references listed Appendix D.

Format and Content of the Resume

As noted above, the resume is your personal marketing device, and it is essential that it be:

(1) *Professional in Appearance.* Your resume should be prepared on a computer and printed on a high-quality laser printer. This will provide a professional appearance *and* make subsequent revisions much easier. Computers also aid in "highlighting" important information. Most universities have computer labs, with technicians to assist you. If *absolutely* necessary, you may use a high-quality electric typewriter, but remember that other applicants will probably be submitting computer-prepared resumes. If possible, individually print each resume. If you decide to make copies, be sure they are *exceptionally* high in quality. Print (or copy) your resume on the quality paper as your cover letter (20# bond with at least 25 percent cotton content). With respect to color, research indicates that most professionals in recreation and leisure studies prefer white, off-white, cream or beige paper.

Note: If you are going to have your resume prepared and/or printed by a commercial company, it is still your responsibility to have the information ready and in the format you desire.

(2) *Clear and Concise.* Your resume should be simple and easy to read. Use words and expressions that are easily understood and express precisely what you want to say. Avoid jargon. Edit your professional resume unmercifully. Eliminate unnecessary words and phrases. Be certain that every piece of information is important and stated as briefly as possible (without violating #3 below).

(3) *Thorough.* Be sure that all relevant information is included. If you are listing items chronologically, do not leave gaps of time that are unexplained. If necessary, your cover letter should be used to explain gaps. Also, be sure to document all important tasks or learning opportunities associated with a given experience. Use "action" verbs to demonstrate your capabilities. A list of action verbs is provided later in this chapter (Figure 5.6, page 99).

(4) *Error Free.* Use every possible means to eliminate errors. Use a computer spell checking program. *Slowly* proofread the resume at least four times. Also, ask a friend or relative who is proficient in English grammar to proofread your resume.

(5) *Balanced and Consistent.* Your resume should be balanced on the page. Too much writing on one side, top or bottom can make the resume appear "lopsided." White spaces (areas not containing text) should also be balanced throughout the resume. Careful attention should be paid to consistency of margins and indentions (e.g., identical margins for headings, uniform indentions within sections). Consistency in wording is important, too.

(6) *The Truth.* The information in your resume should make you look as good as possible, but *not* at the expense of the truth. *Never* lie on a resume, overstate your accomplishments, or mislead a potential internship supervisor regarding your experiences or responsibilities. In the mid 1980's, the then-Director of Tourism for a large eastern city learned this lesson the hard way. She was forced to resign due to questions about the accuracy of information she supplied to a selection committee. Don't let this happen to you! Be selective in what you include in your resume, but be sure it is the truth.

In addition to the information above, there are many things to keep in mind when preparing a professional resume. Some of the more important ones include:

(1) Readers pay the *most* attention to the beginning of a page, paragraph, sentence or list. Therefore, be sure to structure your resume to:

    a. get the most important sections (i.e., professional experiences) toward the front of the resume;

    b. list experiences beginning with the most recent, working back to those in the past; and

    c. give the most relevant responsibilities or skills first.

(2) Do not put personal information such as sex, height, weight, age, or marital status in your resume.

(3) Provide brief descriptions of your professional (and other) work experiences that show skills. Use action verbs.

(4) Make sure words in a series are in the same tense and form. Only use present tense if you are still involved in an activity or work experience. Avoid personal pronouns (e.g., I, me, he, she).

(5) Do not use abbreviations/acronyms by themselves, unless they are *universally* known and accepted (e.g., AIDS, CPR, Postal abbreviations for states). Thus, NRPA should be listed: National Recreation and Park Association (NRPA). In general, contractions should be avoided, too.

(6) Highlight headings and important information by using bold-face type, italics, or underlines, etc. These techniques add emphasis and are important to maintaining good balance on the page.

(7) *Never* print (or copy) a two-page resume back-to-back. Staple (or paper clip) the pages together in the upper left hand corner, and be sure to include your name on page two. Also, make sure the text extends *at least* half-way down page two. If not, expand the text or reduce the resume to one page.

(8) Do not put a page break in the middle of an entry. Also, try to avoid splitting a section (e.g., professional experience) between pages. If you do split a section, be sure to put the heading with "Continued" specified on page two. "Cont'd" is also acceptable, even though it is a contraction.

(9) Generally, it is better *not* to list specific references on an internship resume; rather, indicate that references are available, furnished, or provided upon request. This allows you to select your references, based on the prospective internship agency or supervisor. However, if you print each resume separately, it isn't a problem to list references (especially if you need additional text to complete a two-page resume). Reference information should always be the last item on the resume—it signifies the end of your resume.

Resume Examples

The following pages provide many examples of well-prepared resumes. We begin with a simple straight forward resume format and move to more complex formats for your review. Both one- and two-page resumes are included. These resumes are presented as examples *only*. As mentioned earlier, there is *no* absolutely perfect resume format. Look these resumes over, paying careful attention to both *what* is included and *how* it is presented. We have added comments (see boxes) on some resumes to highlight important aspects. Do not *only* look at the comments, however. Examine each resume thoroughly. Determine what aspects you want to use for your own resume. We have tried to included resumes representing a variety of specializations within the recreation and leisure profession.

The resumes in this manual were done inexpensively because they were prepared on a computer; however, they did take considerable time to construct. You can stay away from expensive commercial resume preparation costs if you have access to a computer with word processing or desktop publishing software. Most of the resumes in this manual were constructed using a Macintosh® SE, with PageMaker® or Microsoft Word® software.

When looking at the different formats in our examples, notice the bold lines, lines used to separate information, and use of other techniques to emphasize specific information. These techniques add emphasis and style to the resume; however, be careful not to overuse such devices. If a resume is considered too "flashy," it may result in a rejection letter.

Michael Smith

100 North Cherry Street
Manaugua, Minnesota 55800
(612) 894-0000

Note balance and
effective use of
white space.

Education

Minnesota State University at Managua
Bachelor of Arts, Recreation Administration: Graduation (DATE)
Option: Resort and Lodging Management
Minor: Business Administration
3.80 overall GPA

Bold type and
varied font size
adds emphasis.

Related Coursework:

Hotel/Resort Management and Development   Resort Programming
Tourism and Travel   Leadership and Supervision
Budgeting and Finance   Resort Marketing
Labor Relations   International Business

Special Project: Student Tour Representative. Conducted feasibility analysis for Overseas Adventures European Travel Company. Helped to organize advertising, marketing, and selling of tour to potential clients. (DATES)

Awards

• Selected as member of Outstanding College Students of America (DATE)
• Five-time Dean's Honor List Student
• Awarded Certificate with Honors from American Hotel and Motel Association by successfully completing Resort Management course with an overall score of 90% or better
• Recipient of $1000 Rollins Merit Award from Minnesota State (DATE)
• Recipient of $4000 Hillsborough Village Scholarship (DATE)

Experience

Recreation Center Program Assistant. Blair House: Minnesota State University at Managua, MN Recruited, selected, and trained Recreation Attendants. Supervised day-to-day activities of nine attendants and seven aerobic instructors. Responsible for collecting aerobic fees and managing center budget. Produced monthly newsletter and provided advertising for all activities. Organized athletic tournaments and leagues. Served as Co-advisor of on-campus Activities Planning Team. (DATES)

Include
internships
and other
course-related
experiences.

Summer Conference Assistant. Student Life: Minnesota State University at Managua, MN Supervised and assigned desk hours to Front Desk Clerks. Organized staff payroll records. Organized and secured facilities as requested by conference groups. Met with conference group leaders and operated as primary contact person for assigned groups. Coordinated meal plans and billing services for conference groups with University Food Service. Assisted and coordinated the check-in and check-out process for groups. Responsible on an "on call" basis. Enforced university policies and confronted violators. (DATES)

Student Intern. Fairfield Lodge and Resort: Fairfield Springs, MN
Implemented planned programs and supervised group activities and special events. Trained in retail sales, bookkeeping and depositing, marketing, safety and liability, and recreation programming. (DATE)

Activities

Member of Student Commercial Recreation Assoication

Interests

Outdoor recreation, physical fitness, and international relations

References

Available upon request

TAMMY S. WILSON

PERMANENT ADDRESS
4203 West Erie
Erie, PA 16000
(814) 000-0000

LOCAL ADDRESS
8607 Wesley
600 East Pennsylvania
Longley, PA 16703
(814) 000-0000

EDUCATION

Bachelor of Science in Recreation and Parks
Longley State University, Longley, PA
Anticipated Graduation: (Date)
Emphasis Area: Therapeutic Recreation
Minor: Psychology
Overall GPA: 3.93/4.00

OTHER EDUCATIONAL EXPERIENCES

Therapeutic Recreation Research and Evaluation: A Seminar for Practitioners, at the Erie State Hospital, Erie, PA
Therapeutic Recreation and Community Re-Entry Programs for Persons with Head Injuries, presentation by Dr. Joanne Alexander from East Coast Rehabilitation Centers, Philadelphia, PA

PROFESSIONAL EXPERIENCE

Children's Rehabilitation Home, Beach City, NJ   DATES

> Specify volunteer and part-time positions.

Position: Independent Study Student (Volunteer)
Responsibilities: Supervised, encouraged, and ensured the safety of patients participating in recreational activities. Documented patient participation as well as incidents witnessed. Also assisted with community outings which involved transferring patients, loading/unloading equipment, driving hospital vehicles, and professionally representing the hospital to the public while protecting individual patients' rights to privacy. In addition, planned and conducted one-on-one sessions with child with a traumatic brain injury, assisted with special physical therapy/therapeutic recreation programs, and helped orient and supervise volunteers.

Position: Receptionist (Part-time)
Responsibilities: Coordinated communication between outside callers and hospital staff by receiving and transmitting calls (including paging hospital personnel) to proper destinations within the hospital. Also provided information and passes for visitors, contacted emergency services when necessary, and professionally represented the hospital to the public.

Position: "Thumper" (Part-time)
Responsibilities: Performed postdural drainage on children with cystic fibrosis. Also documented condition of the child and the characteristics of the expelled mucus.

Office of Disability Services, Erie State, Erie, PA   DATES

Position: Proctor (Part-time)
Responsibilities: Assisted students with disabilities in taking exams (including returning completed exams to instructors).

College Settlement Program, Hollidaysville, PA   DATES

Position: Environmentalist
Responsibilities: Programmed and conducted environmental activities (including spelunking) for inner-city children ages seven through twelve. Also supervised counselors during small group activities.

T. WILSON   Page 2

OTHER EXPERIENCE

Audio Visual Services, Erie State, Erie, PA   DATE - Present

Position: Projectionist (Part-time)
Responsibilities: Cooperating with faculty members to provide audiovisual services for university classes.

Cashew World II, Atlantic City, NJ   DATES

Position: Cashier (Part-time)
Responsibilities: Handled daily receipts and provided information for tourists.

Student Recruitment Task Force, East Comus, PA   DATES

Position: Student Recruiter (Volunteer)
Responsibilities: Planned and conducted presentation designed to recruit high school students for the Erie State University.

Dougal's Restaurant, Kanantus, PA   Summers YEARS

Position: Cashier
Responsibilities: Took orders and handled daily receipts.

> Include expiration
> dates with certificates.

CURRENT CERTIFICATIONS	Advanced First Aid, expires DATE Cardiopulmonary Resuscitation, expires DATE

PROFESSIONAL
INVOLVEMENT
	Helping Hand Program, DATES
	    Assistant Director, DATE - Present.
	Erie State University Recreation and Parks Society,
	    DATE - Present. **Secretary**, DATES.
	Center for Counseling and Psychological Services Advisory Board,
	    DATE - Present. **Co-founder.**
	Interest Group Related to Persons with Disabilities,
	    DATES. **Co-founder.**

> Joining organizations
> demonstrated professional
> commitment.

HONORS	Recreation and Parks YEAR Services Junior Merit Scholarship Award College of Health and Human Development Academic Achievement Scholarship Golden Key National Honor Society Outstanding College Students of America University Scholar's Program, DATES Dean's List, Fall YEAR through Spring YEAR
INTERESTS	Ice skating, repelling, hiking, caving, fishing, canoeing, reading, aerobics.
REFERENCES	Provided on request.

Use of lines may
improve balance
and appearance.

KELLY S. CRAIG

Permanent Address
1 Court Street
Mile High, CO 80621
(303) 267-4000

Present Address
40 West 2nd Avenue, 19F
Thorton, CO 80703
(303) 894-1296

EDUCATION

Mountain State University at Rockies, Rockies, Colorado
Bachelor of Arts, Business Management: Expected (DATE)
Concentration: International Business and Finance

PROFESSIONAL EXPERIENCE

Vice-President. Associated Students, Inc., Mountain State University at Rockies. (DATES) Elected by student body to position of Chief Operating Officer of $14 million, 16,000 member corporation which operates campus bookstore, food services, student government, and student union with a staff of 500 employees. Promoted and facilitated open communication throughout the corporation by effective verbal and written directives and memorandums. Conducted staff assessments. Aided implementation of reorganized managerial structure. Successfully lobbied bill which obtained temporary injunction after a takeover attempt. Additional accomplishments:

- Coordinated extensive recruitment drive that placed 200 students on government boards.

Bullet statements
can emphasize
accomplishments.

- Designed new officer orientation and training program.

- Programmed and budgeted two three-day retreats with a $3,000 budget. Coordinated divergent groups including businesses, management and service components.

- Organized and conducted campus-wide student leadership seminar for 2000 faculty, staff and students. Topics included stress management, fund raising, educational equity, and effective meeting techniques.

Recreation Leader. Western Parks and Recreation Department, Johnson, Colorado. (DATES) Planned and supervised daily activities for youth ages 6 to 16. Designed promotional material including flyers, posters and release forms. Worked effectively with participants, public and agency officials.

Wellness Consultant. Lifestyle Wellness Systems, Mountain State University at Rockies. (DATES) Instructed weekly wellness programs for university students and management level employees for community based commercial organizations. Instructed in areas of time management, stress management, visualization and goal setting.

KELLY S. CRAIG
Page 2

PROFESSIONAL
EXPERIENCE
(continued)

Recreation Leader. Mile High YMCA, Mile High, Colorado. (DATES)
Led overnight and extended stay camps for youth ages 10 to 18. Responsible
for special events at extended stay camps including Farewell Dinner, Counselor
Comedy Night and Fireside Skit Night.

Waitress, Hostess, Cashier. The Noodle House (DATES); Two Guys From
Greece, Mile High, Colorado. (DATES) Greeted customers, received and
placed orders, delivered meals, worked directly with public, co-workers and
management. Responded to a variety of requests quickly, efficently and
accurately under pressure.

AFFILIATIONS

Vice-President Coordinator, Recreation Students Association (DATES)

Founder, Vice-President, Social Director, Generating Developmental Ideas (GDI).
(DATES) Created the largest service and social organization on university's
campus.

Women's Council of the Mountain State University (DATES)

Pledge Class President, Service Chairperson, Alpha Chi Alpha National Sorority
(DATES)

RELATED
ACTIVITIES

President, on-campus residence hall (DATES)
President, Inter-hall President's Council (DATES)
Varsity Diving Team (DATES)
Freshman Orientation Leader (DATES)
Student Academic Affairs Council (DATES)
Student Organization and Activities Council (DATES)
Student Advisory Committee (DATES)

REFERENCES

Available upon request

Christy Marie Lewis

1100 Hobart Street
Razorback, Arkansas 72601
(501) 342-1000

Education

Mississippi Valley University, Razorback, Arkansas
Bachelor of Arts, Psychology and Therapeutic Recreation: Anticipated (DATE)

Related Coursework:

Listing related courses can emphasize areas of expertise.

Leisure Counseling
Therapeutic Case Management
Therapeutic Recreation Techniques
Therapeutic Recreation Services
Wilderness Leadership
Programming for Special Populations
Comprehensive Study of Special Populations

Abnormal Psychology
Social Psychology
Counseling Psychology
Psychology of Prejudice
Drug Use and Abuse
Early Childhood Development
Individual Analysis

Corle College: Corle, California
Associate of Arts, Psychology: DATE

Experience

SMITH DEVELOPMENTAL CENTER, "CAMP VIA": Elderidge, Arkansas
Camp Counselor. Created and implemented daily recreation programs as part of treatment team. Supervised and aided clients in activities of daily living and encouraged socialization. (DATES)

COMMUNITY LIVING CENTER, RIVERSIDE: Paradise, Arkansas
House Counselor. Implemented individualized program plans and supervised clients in daily life skills. Recorded each client's activities and daily programs. Supervised evening recreation group and community interaction group. Assisted clients with conflict resolution. Maintained chart points for day and administered medication. Prepared balanced meals for residents and shopped for groceries. Transported clients to medical appointments and recreation activities. (DATES)

Programmer. Implemented individualized program plans and supervised clients in daily life skills. Led evening recreation group and community interaction group. Served as advocate for clients. Maintained client behavior records. (DATES)

JACK'S RESTAURANT: Lempert, Mississippi
Waitress, Evening Dining Room. Performed customer service. Took orders, added tickets and served food. (DATES)

SAINT THOMAS MEDICAL CENTER: Burton, Arkansas
Secretary/Radiology. Answered phones and transferred calls to appropriate source. Typed forms, memos and various reports. Accepted deliveries. (DATES)

CAMP ABILITY: Westonville, Arkansas
Counselor Aide. Supervised eight campers with developmental disabilities, 6 to 8 years old. Organized group activities. Assisted with behavior management. (DATES)

Christy Marie Lewis
Page 2

Volunteer Experience

SMITH DEVELOPMENTAL CENTER: Elderidge, Arkansas
Organized Community Action Volunteers in Education (CAVE) weekend workshop.
Counselled clients with severe developmental disabilities clients on behavior unit.
(DATES)

MEG TAYLOR'S ADULT DAY PROGRAM: Pendleton, Arkansas
Taught dancing skills to older adults in adaptive dance program. (DATES)

SOCIAL ADVOCATES FOR YOUTH (S.A.Y.): Westbrook, Arkansas
Worked at facility for adolescents with mental illness, including physically and sexually
abused youth. Responsible for implementation of behavior modification program and
enforcement of house policies and procedures. Reviewed individual program plans and
histories. Assisted in case staffings with senior S.A.Y. staff. (DATES)

DEAL DEVELOPMENTAL CENTER: Westbrook, Arkansas
Assisted children with developmental disabilities (6 to 12 years old) with leisure
activities. Worked under the supervision of certified recreational therapist and consultant for North American Health Care Unlimited. (DATES)

LAMPLOC DAY TREATMENT CENTER: Westbrook, Arkansas.
Led recreational activities for youth and adults with mental illnesses. Supervised clients
in meal preparation, ceramics and sports activities. Participated in Group Therapy
sessions led by licensed clinical psychologist. (DATES)

Special Skills and Activities

- Certificate in Wilderness Leadership, Mississippi Valley University
- Cardiopulmonary Resuscitation (CPR). Expires (DATE)
- Advanced First Aid. Expires (DATE)
- Member, Arkansas Park and Recreation Society (APRS)
- Water Safety Instructor (WSI). Expires (DATE)

Interests: Aerobics, backpacking, cross-country skiing, travel (backpacked through
Europe), nutrition, jazz dance, outdoor adventure for persons with disabilities.

Reference

Furnished upon request

Brenda Kathryn Call

729 4th Avenue. • San Francisco, CA • 93000 • (415) 893-7777

Education

San Francisco Bay University, San Francisco, CA
Bachelor of Science, Recreation Administration: Date
    Option: Community and Commercial Recreation
    Minor: Nutrition and Employee Fitness

Related Coursework:

Leadership and Supervision in Recreation	Health Science
Management of Recreation and Parks	Anatomy and Physiology
Introduction to Special Populations	Chemistry and Biochemistry
Foundations Of Programming	Normal Nutrition
Private Enterprise Recreation and Tourism	Therapeutic Nutrition
Recreation Budget and Finance Management	Nutrition Through Life
Computer Programming for Recreation Majors	Nutrition and Physical Fitness
Resort Development and Management	Body Awareness and Weight Control

Experience

KANGAROO KATIE'S FITNESS CENTER: Ellis, California
Pro Shop/Bookkeeping Assistant. Responsible for scheduling reservations, selling food and beverages, and providing clean, rolled towels, plus a friendly welcome upon each member's entrance. Maintained accurate membership records via data entry, performed budget reconciliation and monthly billing procedures, typed and filed documents. (DATES)

SAN FRANCISCO BAY UNIVERSITY, GEOGRAPHY DEPT: San Francisco, California
Secretary. Assisted full-time secretary and worked independently answering and transferring phone calls, typing, Xeroxing, filing, and performing miscellaneous errands. (DATES)

BART'S FITNESS FOR WOMEN: San Francisco, California
Receptionist. Responsible for opening club, selling memberships, and completing contracts, receiving and making phone calls, staffing boutique and preparing billing. Duties also included jacuzzi maintenance, bulletin board displays, miscellaneous signs/posters, and some exercise instruction. (DATES)

ASSOCIATION FOR RETARDED CITIZENS: Westerly, California
Respite Worker/Day Care Aide. Cared for elderly persons with various disabilities in their homes. Tasks included feeding, bathing, toileting, administering medication and providing companionship during leisure activities. Also planned and programmed after school activities for ages 4-10 elementary school children three days per week. (DATES)

RECREATION HOUSE FOR THE HANDICAPPED: Ellis, California
Program Leader Substitute. Assisted in programming and implementing numerous activities mainly in adult day care departments. Duties included supervision of volunteers and implementation of behavior modification techniques. (DATES)

JODY AND ASSOCIATES: Ellis, California
Respite Worker. Provided in-home care for children with disabilities and completed activity reports following every assignment. (DATES)

Experience (Cont'd)

PLEASANTVILLE PARKS AND RECREATION DISTRICT: Pleasantville, California
Gymnastic Coach. Enabled 5-15 year old girls to improve abilities in gymnastics. Coordinated presentations of their talents following each four week session. (DATES)

DORSHALL'S INC: Titus, California
Cashier. Operated cash register for retail clothing chain; named fastest cashier in district. Trained and supervised new employees. (DATES)

Other Information

- Merit Internship Program
- Student Dietetic Association
- Cardiopulmonary Resuscitation (CPR)
- American Sign Language Course
- Competed in the Pan American Games (Gymnastics), Puerto Rico
- Travel experience in Spain, France, U.S. Virgin Islands, Hawaii and Mexico.

Interests

Nutrition and wellness, aerobics, biking, weight training, gymnastics, camping and water-skiing.

References

Thomas E. Johnson, Ph.D.
Department of Recreation and Parks Management
San Francisco Bay University
San Francisco, California 94100
(415) 898-6000

Katie Wells
Manager, Kangaroo Katie's Fitness Center
1026 Skyline Drive
Ellis, California 92001
(415) 895-6000

Scott Azinger
12 N. 8th Street, S.W.
Spokane, Washington 96000
(509) 527-7000

Johnny Pensic
Network System Manager, Instructional Media Center
San Francico Bay University
San Francisco, California 94100
(415) 895-2000

> Listing interests can demonstrate possession of job-related skills.

> If necessary, references can be used to complete two-page resume.

WILLIAM E. WHITE

Current:	**Permanent:**
613 W. 6th St.	12 Common Place
Wilson, NH 03600	Wilson, NH 03600
(603) 342-9000	(603) 487-0000

EDUCATION

New Hampshire State University, Wilson, NH: Graduation (DATE)
B.A. Degree: Information and Communication Studies
      Option: Public Relations
B.A. Degree: Recreation Administration
      Option: Community and Private Enterprise
Overall GPA: 3.95
Outstanding Graduating Senior in Recreation Administration

SKILLS

Budgeting • Purchasing • Desktop Publishing • Leadership

Media Campaign Development • Programming • Word Processing

EXPERIENCE HIGHLIGHTS

COMMISSIONER OF COMMUNICATIONS (DATES)
Active Students, Inc, New Hampshire State University, Wilson, NH
Represented $3 million, 5,000 student corporation
Produced monthly newsletter
Responsible for defining fiscal and operational policies for campus radio station
Directed two campus-wide elections

PUBLIC RELATIONS INTERNSHIP (DATES)
Lifestyle Associates, Wilson, NH
Coordinated media campaign for opening of new business
Developed newspaper, billboard ads and collateral material

PROGRAM ASSISTANT (DATES)
Sweat Fitness Corporation, Mortonville, NH
Assisted in implementation of corporate recreation programs

ROOM RESERVATIONS CLERK (DATES)
Ball Memoriam Union, New Hampshire State University, Wilson, NH
Assisted in room reservations, auto billings and clerical work

ROOM SERVICE ATTENDANT (DATES)
Lake View Inn, Laconia, NH
Room service, banquet set-up and meeting set-up

SPECIAL PROJECTS

Lifestyle Consultant
Co-author of recreation activity book
Organizer of alcohol-free symposium
Academic peer counselor
Campus tour guide

AFFILIATIONS

International Association of Business Communicators
Communications Club, President
Pi Beta Phi National Fraternity

REFERENCES

Provided upon request

EXERCISE TIME!

Now that you have seen some good examples of resumes, let's look at two that contain errors and omissions. The next seven pages (Figures 5.2 through 5.5) provide practice in identifying errors and omissions in resumes. These exercises are identical to the cover letter exercise you completed in Chpater Four. At this point, test your understanding of resumes by circling the errors and missing information in Figure 5.2 and 5.4. Then, check your answers against the errors and omissions we identified (Figures 5.3 and 5.5).

Figure 5.2
Resume Corrections Exercise

Deborah Susan Jeffcoat
750 University Drive
Staunton, CT 06900

INTERNSHIP **OBJECTIVE**	To obtain an internship in the field of Parks and Recreation with an emphasis on Visitor Management and Law Enforcement.

EDUCATION

Bachelor of Science: Recreation and Parks
    Option: Outdoor Recreation
New England University
University City, CT 06913

ACTIVITIES

Student Conservation Club (DATES)
New England University Outing Club (DATES)
    Secretary (DATES)
Connecticut Recreation and Parks Association—Student Branch (DATES)

WORK
EXPERIENCE

(DATE) to Present   Connecticut State Parks
PATROLMAN II   Hilltop Pond State Park
                                     Jacobyville, CT

Responsible for providing public safety through law enforcement action and visitor information. Duties included: Patroling park, campground, beaches, and nearby boat landings and waterways; keeping daily logs and records, assisting public with information, first aid, and emergency situations; and maintaining equipment and facilities. Successfully completed Connecticut State Parks law enforcement training.

(DATES)   Blueberry Fields, Inc.
RESIDENTIAL COUNSELOR   West Chester,VT

Responsible for instruction and supervision of children and adults with mental disabilities. Duties included: Assisting in daily living skills; counseling clients in areas of personal development, socialization, and coping skills; maintaining daily logs; and participating in staff meetings, etc.

(DATES)   City of Hillsdale
TRAIL SUPERVISOR   Goode Environmental Area
(Volunteer)   Hillsdale, VT

Responsible for trail maintenance. Duties included: Supervision of teenage volunteer staff; conducting periodic inspections of designated trails; and maintaining records on designated trails.

Figure 5.2
Resume Corrections Exercise (continued)

Page 2

WORK
EXPERIENCE

(DATES)
CLERK (Part-time)

Curriculum Materials Center
New England University
University City, CT

Responsible for front desk operations. Duties included: Providing information; arranging and locating reserve materials; assisting students; and shelving resources. Also assisted in typing, labeling, and designing display cases.

(DATES)
FOREST SERVICE VOLUNTEER Manstone National Forest

USDA Forest Service

Duties included patrolling campsites and river landings, providing visitor information and ensuring good public relations, and maintaining trails. Also assisted in law enforcement, front desk, office duties, and map work. Conducted tours for school-age children. Qualified as National Forest Firefighter.

(DATES)
CANVASSER

Public Interest Coalition
Inquiry, CT

Duties included: Presenting information on important economic and political issues to the public; requesting donations; and training new employees. Also attended relevant workshops and training sessions.

CERTIFICATIONS Advanced First Aid and Emergency Care
Cardiopulmonary Resuscitation (CPR)
Red Card—National Forest Firefighter

PERSONAL DATA Height: 5' 6"
Weight: 125 lbs.
Marital Status: Single
Health: Excellent

REFERENCES Available upon request

Figure 5.3
Resume Corrections Exercise

Optional, but cover letter is better place for objective.

INTERNSHIP OBJECTIVE

EDUCATION

ACTIVITIES

Place below more important categories.

WORK EXPERIENCE

Use present tense for on-going experiences.

Deborah Susan Jeffcoat

750 University Drive
Staunton, CT 06900

Include phone number.

To obtain an internship in the field of Parks and Recreation with an emphasis on Visitor Management and Law Enforcement.

Bachelor of Science: Recreation and Parks
    Option: Outdoor Recreation
New England University
University City, CT 06913

Give expected graduation date (Month, Year).

Student Conservation Club (DATES)
New England University Outing Club (DATES)
    Secretary (DATES)
Connecticut Recreation and Parks Association—Student Branch (DATES)

(DATE) to Present   Connecticut State Parks
PATROLMAN II   Hilltop Pond State Park
                                     Jacobyville, CT

Misspelled word.

Responsible for providing public safety through law enforcement action and visitor information. Duties included: Patroling park, campground, beaches, and nearby boat landings and waterways; keeping daily logs and records, assisting public with information, first aid, and emergency situations; and maintaining equipment and facilities. Successfully completed Connecticut State Parks law enforcement training.

(DATES)   Blueberry Fields, Inc.
RESIDENTIAL COUNSELOR   West Chester, VT

Responsible for instruction and supervision of children and adults with mental disabilities. Duties included: Assisting in daily living skills; counseling clients in areas of personal development, socialization, and coping skills; maintaining daily logs; and participating in staff meetings, etc.

No not use etcetera, and avoid use of abbreviations.

(DATES)   City of Hillsdale
TRAIL SUPERVISOR   Goode Environmental Area
(Volunteer)   Hillsdale, VT

Responsible for trail maintenance. Duties included: Supervision of teenage volunteer staff; conducting periodic inspections of designated trails; and maintaining records on designated trails.

Figure 5.3
Resume Corrections Exercise (continued)

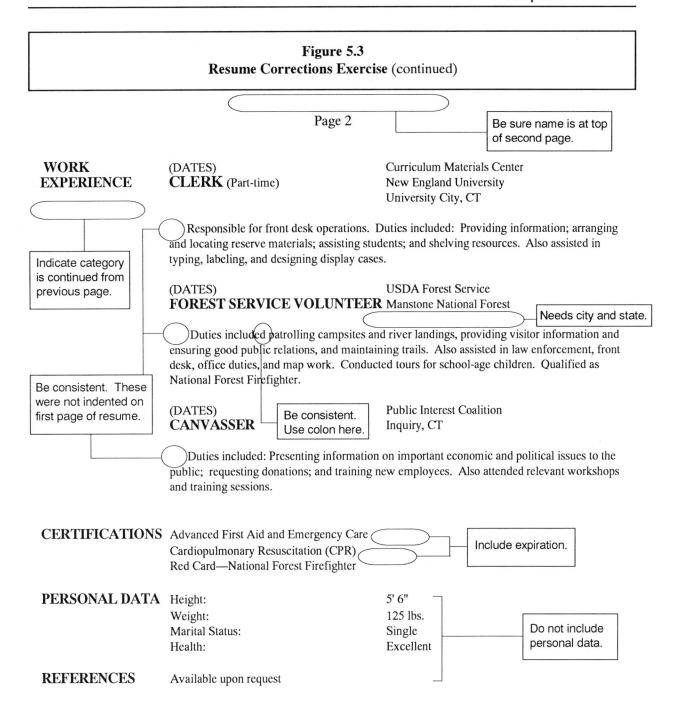

Page 2

Be sure name is at top of second page.

WORK EXPERIENCE   (DATES)   **CLERK** (Part-time)   Curriculum Materials Center
New England University
University City, CT

Indicate category is continued from previous page.

Responsible for front desk operations. Duties included: Providing information; arranging and locating reserve materials; assisting students; and shelving resources. Also assisted in typing, labeling, and designing display cases.

(DATES)   USDA Forest Service
FOREST SERVICE VOLUNTEER Manstone National Forest

Needs city and state.

Duties included patrolling campsites and river landings, providing visitor information and ensuring good public relations, and maintaining trails. Also assisted in law enforcement, front desk, office duties, and map work. Conducted tours for school-age children. Qualified as National Forest Firefighter.

Be consistent. These were not indented on first page of resume.

(DATES)   Public Interest Coalition
CANVASSER   Be consistent. Use colon here.   Inquiry, CT

Duties included: Presenting information on important economic and political issues to the public; requesting donations; and training new employees. Also attended relevant workshops and training sessions.

CERTIFICATIONS   Advanced First Aid and Emergency Care
Cardiopulmonary Resuscitation (CPR)
Red Card—National Forest Firefighter

Include expiration.

PERSONAL DATA   Height: 5' 6"
Weight: 125 lbs.
Marital Status: Single
Health: Excellent

Do not include personal data.

REFERENCES   Available upon request

Figure 5.4
Resume Corrections Exercise

WILLIAM PEPPER

2000 North Hollen Way   San Jose, CA 94128   (408) 722-1200

EDUCATION

Leland Surfer University, San Jose, CA
B.S. Degree: (DATE)
Minor: Gerontology
Anticipated Graduation: (DATE)

Related Coursework:

Anatomy	Programming for Special Populations
Physiology	Leisure Counseling
Social Gerontology	Therapeutic Recreation Services
College Algebra	Therapeutic Recreation Techniques
Aging and Leisure	Therapeutic Case Management

EXPERIENCE

Sierra Home and Village, San Diego, CA   January 1992 to Present
Therapeutic Recreation Director: Responsible for providing therapeutic recreation and
social programming for complex of 200 adult residents. Duties: I assess needs, develop
and implement programs, meet with medical staff, attend team meetings, and provide
community awareness. Also supervise staff of 3 TR assistants and trained volunteers.

Lynbrook Community Center, Lynbrook, CA   March 1989 to March 1990
Recreation Coordinator: Responsible for program development and implementation for older adults
in a community setting. Duties: I scheduled activities and entertainment, provided community
awareness training, coordinated community outings, and trained volunteers.

Hartswick Veterans Home, Hartswick, CA   April 1990 to January 1992
Recreation Supervisor: Responsible for therapeutic recreation programming for residents within
medical treatment program. Duties: I conducted assessments through interviews and observations,
charted progress of residents, evaluated effectiveness of programs, initiated appropriate referrals, and
participated in interdisciplinary team meetings. Also supervised staff of 5 technicians and trained
volunteers.

Broughton City Parks and Recreation, Broughton, CA   Summers 1987, 1988
Recreation Leader: Responsible for providing community recreation for people with special needs.
Duties: I coordinated and supervised special events, community trips, leisure awareness classes, and
socialization training.

CERTIFICATIONS

Multi-Media Standard First Aid (Expiration: DATE)
Therapeutic Recreation Specialist, California Board of Park and Recreation Personnel

---

REFERENCES

Available upon request

Figure 5.5
Resume Corrections Exercise (continued)

WILLIAM PEPPER

2000 North Hollen Way   San Jose, CA 94128   (408) 722-1200

EDUCATION

Leland Surfer University, San Jose, CA
B.S. Degree: Recreation Administration (DATE)
Minor: Gerontology
Anticipated Graduation: (DATE)

> Include city and state of university, plus major.

> Include only courses related to major and option/emphasis.

Related Coursework:

Anatomy   Programming for Special Populations
Physiology   Leisure Counseling
Social Gerontology   Therapeutic Recreation Services
College Algebra   Therapeutic Recreation Techniques
Aging and Leisure   Therapeutic Case Management

EXPERIENCE

Sierra Home and Village, San Diego, CA   January 1992 to Present
Therapeutic Recreation Director: Responsible for providing therapeutic recreation and social programming for complex of 200 adult residents. Duties: I assess needs, develop and implement programs, meet with medical staff, attend team meetings, and provide community awareness. Also supervise staff of 3 TR assistants and trained volunteers.

> Experiences are out of order. List entries in reverse chronological order.

Lynbrook Community Center, Lynbrook, CA   March 1989 to March 1990
Recreation Coordinator: Responsible for program development and implementation for older adults in a community setting. Duties: I scheduled activities and entertainment, provided community awareness training, coordinated community outings, and trained volunteers.

Hartswick Veterans Home, Hartswick, CA   April 1990 to January 1992
Recreation Supervisor: Responsible for therapeutic recreation programming for residents within medical treatment program. Duties: I conducted assessments through interviews and observations, charted progress of residents, evaluated effectiveness of programs, initiated appropriate referrals, and participated in interdisciplinary team meetings. I Also supervised staff of 5 technicians and trained volunteers.

> Do not use personal pronoun.

Broughton City Parks and Recreation, Broughton, CA   Summers 1987, 1988
Recreation Leader: Responsible for providing community recreation for people with special needs. Duties: Special events, community trips, leisure awareness classes, and socialization training.

CERTIFICATIONS

> Need action verbs here.

Multi-Media Standard First Aid (Expiration: DATE)
Therapeutic Recreation Specialist, California Board of Park and Recreation Personnel

---

REFERENCES

Available upon request

Additional Comments on Resumes

Commercial Resume Preparation and Printing

If you do not have access to a computer and laser printer, you may decide to use a commercial resume service or printing firm. Here are some tips on having your materials commercially prepared:

(1) Check out the commercial service or printer first. Ask to see resumes they have printed for other people (most printers keep copies of resumes they produce).

(2) Check out the service or printer's prices (e.g., preparation estimates, printing, quality of paper, paper colors, quantity price, ability to make simple changes).

(4) The service or printer should provide you with a proof for your review. When you receive the proof, make certain you check it over (at least four times!) for misspelled words or other errors. Have others check it, too. Printers will not usually change a resume once it is printed if *you* missed a mistake. Once you initial the proof for printing, the responsibility for errors has shifted to you and not the printer.

(5) Remember to check your completed resume before you leave the service or printer's place of business. Is the format proper? Is the print dark? Is the quality of paper what you specified?

(6) **Important!** Make certain the service or printer respects your wishes and does not reproduce your resume from an "assembly line" approach. You don't want your resume to look like everyone else's! Printers must respect your wishes because it is your money you are spending. Be assertive, if necessary! Make sure you get the resume you want.

References

You must have at least three references, but try to identify more than three. Ask permission from each person to use his or her name as a reference. You many even want to provide each reference with an updated resume. Who should you select as references?

(1) A past employer (or volunteer coordinator) who knows your work skills, leadership potential, reliability, and work ethic.

(2) An educator who knows your academic abilities, social skills, and your ability to work on your own, as well as work with others.

(3) A past or present friend/acquaintance, *not a relative or peer,* who knows your personal character, trustworthiness, and positive behaviors. It is generally best to select someone who is an established professional or family person (e.g., parent of a friend, member of the clergy, recreation leader).

You may list more than three references, but we suggest that you not include any more than four in your reference list. If you have additional references, keep them available on a separate sheet of paper because some agencies may ask for additional references not stated on your resume. Additional references can be in any of the three areas described above, and you may decide to use more than one in a given area.

If your references are not included on your resume, they should be listed on a separate sheet of paper. The rules for preparing your reference list are the same as the rules for your resume (i.e., professional appearance, well-balanced on page, high-quality paper). Each reference should be printed or typed in block form and include the person's full name, title (if appropriate), complete mailing address and zip code, and telephone area code and number. Generally, a work address is preferred because most reference checks are done during the workday.

Position Requirements

Are there any prerequisites or requirements necessary to qualify for the internship position you want? If certificates (e.g., CPR, Water Safety Instructor) or specific courses are required, make sure you include these qualifications in your cover letter and resume. If you do not possess the necessary prerequisites or requirements, you need to find out how to obtain these documents or courses. Try to meet all requirements before applying even though some agencies will allow an intern to start the internship while he or she is taking a prerequisite course or certificate program.

Answering Machine

An answering machine can be a useful tool in your internship search. This allows potential internship supervisors to contact you even while you are away from the phone. Some people do not like answering machines, so make your introductory message brief, positive and, most of all, appropriate. Having a prospective internship supervisor call your answering machine when you have a jingle or silly message on it may destroy your chances for the internship you want!

Final Comment

It is now time for you to begin constructing your *own* resume, and the pages that follow are intended to help you in this process. Page 99 gives a list of action verbs (Figure 5.6). Page 100 offers a Resume Guide (Figure 5.7) to assist you. Once you have completed a draft of your resume, use the Resume Checklist on page 101 (Figure 5.8) to ensure that your resume conforms to the suggestions in this manual.

In preparing your resume, you should refer to the many examples in this chapter; however, remember that your resume is a reflection of *you*. Construct your resume using your own wording, and select a format, type (font), and style that presents a professional image. The result should be a resume you are proud of—and one that gets you the internship interview you want.

Figure 5.6
Action Verbs for Use in Resumes

Below is a list of "action" verbs that indicate to a prospective internship supervisor (or employer) that you are a person who gets things done. Also, using a variety of these verbs in your resume demonstrates diverse skills, knowledge and abilities.

Go through this list and circle those that you want to include in your resume. Pay particular attention to verbs that are critical to success in your area of specialization. You may also want to add some verbs of your own.

Analyzed	Distributed	Organized
Administered	Documented	Performed
Advanced	Edited	Planned
Advocated	Educated	Prepared
Advised	Eliminated	Presented
Analyzed	Established	Processed
Arranged	Evaluated	Produced
Assessed	Expanded	Promoted
Assisted	Founded	Purchased
Built	Hired	Recommended
Charted	Identified	Reduced
Coached	Implemented	Represented
Collected	Improved	Researched
Completed	Increased	Restored
Conceptualized	Initiated	Restructured
Conducted	Installed	Saved
Conserved	Instituted	Scheduled
Consulted	Instructed	Selected
Contracted	Interpreted	Served
Controlled	Interviewed	Sold
Coordinated	Introduced	Solved
Counseled	Inventoried	Studied
Created	Led	Supervised
Decreased	Maintained	Taught
Designed	Managed	Tested
Determined	Negotiated	Trained
Developed	Obtained	Wrote
Directed	Operated	

Figure 5.7
Resume Guide

---

1. *Heading:* Name, current address, day and night phone. If your current address is temporary, you may want to list your permanent address, as well.

2. *Career objective* (optional): This can be covered more extensively in your cover letter, and including it may limit the use of your resume.

3. *Education* (i.e., community college, college, university): Generally, high school should not be listed. Optional: You may also want to put a list of courses you have taken that are relevant to your major and specialization.

4. *Work and/or volunteer experience:* This category is often divided into two sections (e.g., paid and volunteer, professional and other work). Dividing this category may help you get the most important experiences at the beginning of a section. However, do not divide the category if a section is limited to only one experience. Describe the experience according to the skills that you demonstrated in the position. Use action verbs to create action phrases. Make the experiences sound like they belong to you—that you actually did them and did them *well.*

5. *Skill areas/accomplishments* (optional): An easy to read listing of your skills and accomplishments may be useful to emphasize your abilities. This can be an important area, especially if your work and/or volunteer history is limited. Profession-related service may also be listed here.

6. *Awards, honors, certificates, licenses:* Remember not to abbreviate or use acronyms. List the entire title, with the abbreviated title in parentheses.

Note: The order of categories #3 through #6 is sometimes changed, depending upon what the applicant wants to emphasize. Most professionals expect to see education first, however.

7. *Memberships* (community/campus organizations, professional associations): Be sure to list offices held and responsibilities.

8. *Interests and hobbies:* Some companies like to see that their employees have interests away from work; it demonstrates a balance of life. Also, this section can show you have skills important to a recreation/leisure service professional.

9. *References:* Leaving references off helps you to target specific references for specific agencies or supervisors. We prefer "References (available) (furnished) (provided) upon request."

Figure 5.8
Resume Checklist

Check Off:

_____ Material fits neatly on one or two pages. If two pages, at least 1/2 of second page is filled with text. Also, the top of page two includes name and the text begins with a new entry.

_____ Overall appearance is balanced (*both* pages, if two-page resume), including adequate white space at top, bottom, sides and between entries.

_____ No spelling, grammatical, or punctuation errors.

_____ Printing or typing is neat, clean, and looks professional.

_____ Name, address(es), and telephone number(s) are at the top.

_____ Writing style is concise and direct. Information is easy to read.

_____ Abbreviations or acronyms, if used, are in parentheses and preceded by full title. Contractions and personal pronouns (e.g., I, me, my) are not used.

_____ Paragraph information is brief, to the point, and complete.

_____ Words in a series are in the same tense and form.

_____ All appropriate education, work experiences, skills, etc. are included in the resume.

_____ Important titles are emphasized by bold print or underlined, where appropriate, but these techniques are not overused.

_____ Indentions are appropriately used to set off information and create eye appeal. Indention locations are uniform within sections.

_____ Accomplishments and experiences are described using action verbs to create action phrases.

_____ Dates are uniform, with no big gaps.

_____ Personal data (sex, height, age, marital status, etc.) is *not* included.

_____ Overall resume demonstrates your ability to produce results.

Also have other people check your resume using this form!

SUMMARY

The information in this chapter, and the preceding one, is presented to help you design the tools (i.e., cover letter and resume) necessary for applying for an internship. Exercises and examples are provided for your use and information. Use these exercises and examples, plus your own knowledge, to develop the tools that will work best for you. Remember, these tools represent you, and are usually the first examples of your work that a potential internship supervisor sees. Make them represent the *best* you.

Now that you have prepared high-quality tools and have shown the best you, it is the potential internship supervisor's turn to evaluate how well you match his or her agency's needs. If all goes well, the next aspect of the internship process should be the interview. Chapter Six provides many excellent tips on how to be ready for that big day.

Interview

"There is always one moment . . . when the door opens and lets the future in."
—Graham Greene

When preparing for an internship, nothing causes more stress than the idea of going through an interview. If you are like most students, you do not have a lot of experience with interviews. Therefore, you have concerns about how to dress, how to act, what you might be asked, and what to say during an interview. This chapter will help you cope with these and other concerns prior to, during, and after the internship interview.

To prepare for an interview, you must:

• Develop the proper frame of mind,

• Do your homework, and

• Practice, practice, practice.

When participating in an interview, you should:

• Know the different types of interviews,

• Display professionalism during the interview, and

• Follow-up after the interview.

PREPARING FOR AN INTERVIEW

Developing the Proper Frame of Mind

First, it is important to understand that an internship interview is a *two*-way process. You are, of course, being evaluated by the interviewer, but you are also evaluating whether this agency and agency supervisor are "right" for you. Recognizing that you are an equal participant in the interview process is essential—it will help give you confidence and ensure that you are in the proper frame of mind throughout the interview. You are not a helpless pawn in the interview process. Ultimately, *you* have control over whether you decide to do your internship with the interviewer's agency.

Chapter One (Self-Assessment) helped you develop positive "self-talk." At this point, quickly review the information on pages 3 to 5. The foundation of a successful interview is to think positively and project a confident, professional image.

Doing Your Homework

Being successful during interviews does not just happen. It takes a lot of hard work to prepare for an interview, including attending to logistical concerns, reviewing data about the agency, reviewing your self assessment, preparing answers to questions you might be asked, and preparing questions that you want to ask.

Logistical Concerns

There are a lot of logistical things to keep in mind as you prepare for an interview. For example, you need to know exactly how to get to the interview site, and how long it will take to get there. If the interview site is in a busy area, you should plan an alternative route in case of traffic delays. Additional logistical concerns include having an extra copy of your resume to take with you, selecting and preparing the clothes you plan to wear, writing or calling to confirm the interview, preparing a portfolio, and making sure you have enough change for making a phone call or for parking. Some of these things may seem trivial, but overlooking a minor item can sometimes cause a major problem.

We suggest that you take the time to put logistical information in a checklist format. Thus, preliminary items will become routine, allowing you to concentrate on other aspects of the interview process. The following page (Figure 6.1) gives you an example of an "Interview Logistics Checklist." Under pressure, everyone has a tendency to forget important things. Use the Interview Logistics Checklist as a reminder of what you need to do, as well as what you need to take with you to the interview. Also, remember to add necessary items to the Interview Logistics Checklist, as you identify them.

Most of the information on the checklist is self explanatory, but a couple of logistical items should be discussed. These are:

Confirmation Letter or Call. There are few experiences more embarrassing than arriving at an interview site at the wrong day or time. Therefore, a few days before your appointed interview, you should confirm the date, time and location of your interview. This may be done by letter or, if you prefer, by phone. Confirming your appointment by phone also gives you the chance to ask for directions, if needed, and clarify parking arrangements.

Practice Trip to Interview Location. If you are not familiar with the location of your interview site, how to get there, or the traffic patterns in the area, we suggest you take a practice trip in advance of the interview date. It is essential to arrive on time for an interview; therefore, you need to know *exactly* where you are going and how long it will take you to get there. If heavy traffic is a problem, be sure to do your practice trip at the same time of day as your interview. Also, be sure to practice your alternative route.

The Portfolio. A portfolio is usually a binder or large envelope/briefcase containing samples of your work. The best example of a portfolio is one that a "model" takes to job interviews. In the portfolio is a variety of photographs—close-ups, formal dress, casual dress, etc., designed to show both modeling skill and versatility. Like a model, you probably have things you have accomplished that demonstrate your skill and versatility. Possible portfolio items include things you have written or developed in school or at a job, such as business letters, scholarly papers, brochures, and promotional fliers. Some specializations within recreation and leisure services (e.g., marketing in commercial recreation) lend themselves well to the use of a portfolio. You might offer your portfolio during the interview or even at the end of the interview, but do *not* force the portfolio on the interviewer. Let him or her know it exists and be ready to show it with pride.

Figure 6.1
Interview Logistics Checklist

Agency Name, Address, Phone and Contact Person:

_____

_____

_____

Part I. Advance Preparation

Check Off:

____ Set date of interview: _____

____ Set time of interview: _____

____ Set location of interview: _____

____ Identify person to report to: _____

____ Write or call to confirm interview (inc. time/date/location) _____

____ Secure map to interview location

____ Determine best route to interview location

____ Identify alternative route, if needed

____ Take "practice" trip to interview location, if possible

____ Make extra copy of resume

____ Complete employment application, if needed

____ Make extra copy of reference letters, if appropriate

____ Prepare portfolio, if appropriate

____ Select clothes and accessories (jewelry, etc.)

____ Prepare clothes (cleaning, washing, pressing, shining shoes, etc.)

_____

_____

Part II. Things to take

____ Interviewers name and phone number _____

____ Change for telephone and parking

____ Map to interview location (including precise address of location)

____ Copy of resume (plus reference letters and/or employment application, if appropriate)

____ Portfolio (if appropriate)

____ Agency brochures, interview notes, etc. (to review prior to interview)

_____

_____

Reviewing Agency Data. Chapter Three (Research) helped you to identify ways to gather detailed information on potential internship agencies. Before an interview, it is essential to review this information. An interviewer will probably be impressed if you demonstrate knowledge of his or her agency. Also, reviewing agency data will help you prepare insightful questions to use during the interview.

Reviewing Your Self-Assessment. Chapter One (Self-Assessment) provided information and exercises to help you understand yourself more thoroughly. The interview gives you a chance to put this information into action. One of the things interviewers will look for during an interview is whether or not you understand yourself and your own capabilities. Reviewing the forms on pages 9 through 11 is excellent preparation for an interview.

Preparing Answers to Potential Questions. Usually you will not know in advance the questions that will be asked during your interview. Nevertheless, you *can* prepare for interview questions. One way is to check with your classmates. Have any of them interviewed with the agency? If so, ask for their advice, with particular attention to questions they were asked during the interview. One question most internship interviewers ask is, "What does your university expect from your agency supervisor?" Be sure that you know your university's expectations regarding paperwork, interns' evaluations, conferences with faculty members, etc. You should also carefully review questions that are commonly asked during internship interviews and prepare answers to as many as possible.

EXERCISE TIME!

Figure 6.2 provides a list of thirty interview questions that are frequently asked of potential interns. Taking the time now to answer each of these questions may relieve you of a great deal of stress and tension later. Review each question and write down your answer in the space provided. Be thorough, but concise. After you have finished writing down your answers, give some thought to "Other Potential Questions" and "Situational Questions" listed at the end of Figure 6.2, page 112.

Figure 6.2
Internship Interview Questions

The following are questions that are frequently asked of interns during an interview. Read each question, then use the space provided to formulate your answer. The purpose of this exercise is not to have you memorize your answers; rather, it is to help you think through your responses in advance. Then, if one of these questions is asked during your interview, you will be able to respond in a relaxed and natural manner. Remember to keep your answers brief but thorough.

1.   What are your short- and long-range goals, and how are you preparing to reach them?

2.   Why did you choose this career, and what do you want to gain from it?

3.   What do you consider to be your strengths and weaknesses?

4.   How would you describe yourself?

5.   How do you think past employers would evaluate you and your performance?

Figure 6.2 (continued)

6.   How do you think your professors would describe you?

_____

_____

_____

_____

7.   Why should I take you as an intern?

_____

_____

_____

_____

8.   How do you function under pressure?

_____

_____

_____

_____

9.   What things have you learned in school that will help you as an intern?

_____

_____

_____

_____

10.   Why did you decide to seek an internship with this agency?

_____

_____

_____

_____

11.   Describe your past experiences that relate to the type of internship position you are seeking?

_____

_____

_____

_____

Figure 6.2 (continued)

12.   Describe a mistake you have made in your life and tell me what you learned from it?

_____

_____

_____

_____

13.   How do you define success?

_____

_____

_____

_____

14.   What qualities do you think a good internship supervisor should have?

_____

_____

_____

_____

15.   What qualities do you think a good intern should have?

_____

_____

_____

_____

16.   What are you doing to keep up to date with your field?

_____

_____

_____

_____

17.   Describe a problem that you have faced and tell me how you solved it. What did you learn from this experience?

_____

_____

_____

_____

Figure 6.2 (continued)

18.   How are your written communication skills?

_____

_____

_____

_____

19.   Why do you feel you are qualified for an internship position?

_____

_____

_____

_____

20.   What are the three most important things you have learned from your formal education?

_____

_____

_____

_____

21.   What are your greatest concerns about starting your internship?

_____

_____

_____

_____

22.   Do your grades show your true potential? If not, why not?

_____

_____

_____

_____

23.   What are your greatest accomplishments to date?

_____

_____

_____

_____

Figure 6.2 (continued)

24. What are the two or three things most important to you in selecting your internship site?

_____

_____

_____

_____

25. What experiences do you have speaking before groups and how well did you perform?

_____

_____

_____

_____

26. What do you find most satisfying in a job?

_____

_____

_____

_____

27. What experiences do you have with computers?

_____

_____

_____

_____

28. Would you describe yourself as an ethical person? If so, why?

_____

_____

_____

_____

29. Describe a discipline problem you have had to handle. How did you deal with it?

_____

_____

_____

_____

Figure 6.2 (continued)

30.   What things do you do to motivate yourself?

_____

_____

_____

_____

Other potential questions:

What skills and abilities do you bring to your internship?

Why did you select (your university)?

What organizations do you belong to?

What has been your most interesting job? Why?

What has been your least interesting job? Why?

If you were me, would you select yourself for this internship? Why?

What skills do you think are crucial for an intern to possess?

What do you know about this agency?

Do you like to travel? Why?

What do you see yourself doing five years from now?

What are your hobbies and interests?

What types of books do you read for pleasure? Tell me about one of them.

Situational questions:

You should also be prepared to answer situational questions (i.e., those questions where you are given a situation and asked to react to it). Remember, however, that most agencies already have policies and procedures set up for many routine situations. If you think a policy might exist, consider prefacing your answer by saying, "If the agency has an established policy for handling this situation, I would follow it. If not, I would . . . " The following are some examples of situational questions:

You have worked hard preparing a promotional brochure for the agency, but another intern shows it to your supervisor and takes credit for your work. What would you do?

You take a group of individuals with head injuries on a community outing. During the trip, one of your clients makes an inappropriate sexual advance toward you. How would you react to the advance and what would you do after returning to the agency?

You are working on a project with two other interns. As the project progresses, you become aware that one of the interns is violating company policy by taking agency materials for personal use. What would you do?

Overtime, you become convinced that a child in one of your recreation programs is the victim of child abuse. Should you do anything about your suspicions? If so, what?

You are leading an activity for teenagers in our nature center. During the session, you hear one of the teenagers make a racist remark. The purpose of your session is environmental awareness, not race relations, and no members of the racial group in question are present. What, if anything, should you do?

Preparing Questions You Want to Ask

As mentioned above, the internship interview is a two-way process. Not only does the interviewer need to decide if the agency wants you as an intern, but you have to decide if this agency offers the internship experience you want. You should not leave the interview without knowing the answers to the following questions:

- Who will be your direct supervisor?
- Has the agency had interns before?
- Has your direct supervisor had experience supervising interns?
- What work schedule will you be expected to maintain (days/hours)?
- What will be your primary duties and responsibilities?
- What will be the nature of your orientation upon arrival?
- What are the possibilities of job opportunities with the agency (only if you hope to work there aftergraduation)?
- Do interns receive a stipend or salary (only if important to selection of your internship agency)?
- Does the agency have any special requirements or policies regarding interns (e.g., attire, policies on visitors)?
- Can you meet your educational goals as an intern with the agency?
- How are interns evaluated?
- When will a decision about your internship application be made, and how it will be communicated to you?

Generally, most of the above information will be given to you without asking. If, however, some of these items are not covered by your interviewer, you must be prepared to ask questions. When asking questions, it is important to emphasize aspects of the internship that are important to your educational goals and career development. Do *not* ask trivial questions or questions that have obvious answers. Use the above list, plus other information that you want to learn during the interview, to develop a list of questions that you might ask during your interview.

EXERCISE TIME!

Use the following page (Figure 6.3) to write down the questions you want to ask an interviewer.

Figure 6.3
Questions to Ask an Interviewer

In the space provided, list ten (10) questions that you might ask an interviewer. Arrange your questions from most important (#1) to least important (#10).

Question #1: _____
_____
_____

Question #2: _____
_____
_____

Question #3: _____
_____
_____

Question #4: _____
_____
_____

Question #5: _____
_____
_____

Question #6: _____
_____
_____

Question #7: _____
_____
_____

Question #8: _____
_____
_____

Question #9: _____
_____
_____

Question #10: _____
_____
_____

Practice, Practice, Practice

The final step in preparing for an internship interview is to practice your interviewing skills . . . over and over again. Like most skills, answering questions in an interview situation does not come naturally. It takes practice to learn how to relax and answer difficult questions with ease and confidence. It takes practice to learn how to ask important questions of an interviewer without sounding either defensive or aggressive. It also takes practice to eliminate annoying mannerisms or distracting movements during an interview situation.

But, exactly how can you practice your interviewing skills? One of the most effective ways is to participate in "mock" interviews. Start by asking a friend or relative to interview you. Pretend you are in a real interview situation and have the friend or relative ask you questions from Figure 6.2. This will give you practice in verbalizing answers that you have already put on paper. Moreover, it will enable you to start practicing your interviewing skills in a very nonthreatening environment. If possible, videotape your mock interview, then sit down and discuss what things you did well and what areas still need work. Pay particular attention to such things as distracting mannerisms, poor grammar, and verbal fillers ("uhmms").

Next, ask a *different* friend or relative to interview you, only this time have him or her develop the questions. This may give you practice in responding to questions you have not thought about before. Again, after the mock interview is over, process the interview to identify your strengths and weaknesses. If the staff members at your university's career development center conducts mock interviews, also interview with them and have them evaluate your skills. Although these individuals may not have in-depth knowledge about recreation and leisure services, they are experts in interviewing techniques.

Finally, after you feel comfortable with your interviewing skills, it is time to participate in the real thing— an internship interview. If you have a "first choice" agency, we suggest that you *not* interview with this agency until you have interviewed at one or two other potential agencies. Thus, by the time you interview at the agency you want most, your interviewing skills should be at their peak.

PARTICIPATING IN AN INTERVIEW

Types of Internship Interviews

It is difficult to predict exactly how an internship interview will be conducted. Most of the time, internship interviews are one-to-one; however, sometimes more than one staff member will interview you. Generally, an interviewer will want to show you around the agency and familiarize you with its departments and services. This may take place before or after a formal questioning period; however, important interview questions may also be asked *while* you are being shown around the agency. Remember you are applying for an internship, not a full-time job. Try to relax and be prepared for any type of interview.

Sometimes interviewers are so anxious to have student interns that they do not even conduct a formal interview. Rather, they use the interview time to "sell" their agency to the student. If this happens to you, do not forget that *you* have lots of questions that need to be answered. Even if someone chooses not to interview you, make sure you still get your questions answered.

If a formal interview is held, it will usually go through three stages. These are:

1. *Breaking the ice.* In this stage, the interviewer will generally try to make you comfortable in the interview situation. Nonthreatening topics are usually discussed, such as the weather, local sports, or your university. If other interviewers are present, they will usually be introduced and their roles explained during this stage.

2. *Inquiry.* This is the stage where the interviewer asks specific questions of you. Generally, these questions are designed to find out what kind of a person you are and what kind of an intern you will be. Providing you have done a good job of preparing, this stage should not produce anxiety for you. This is also the stage where you ask your questions of the interviewer.

3. *Conclusion.* At this stage, the interviewer controls the ending of the interview and lets you know what happens next (i.e., when a decision will be made and how you will be notified). It also provides a final chance for either you or the interviewer to get clarification on any aspect of the interview process.

On rare occasions, a "second" internship interview is held. This requires a potential intern to return for another interview. This second interview is generally more in-depth than the first one, and usually means that there is stiff competition for an internship position. Situational questions (see Figure 6.2) are sometimes saved for a second interview.

Internship interviews, unlike most job interviews, are sometimes conducted by telephone. Often, a student who wishes to do his or her internship a great distance from school and home cannot afford the time or expense to travel to agency's location just for an interview. Thus, it becomes necessary to conduct a telephone interview. Telephone interviews may seem to be less threatening than face-to-face interviews because the student's concerns about proper attire, distracting mannerisms, etc., are eliminated. However, telephone interviews do not allow a student to demonstrate

his or her professionalism and enthusiasm through such details as proper dress and good use of nonverbal communication. Voice quality, voice inflection, grammar, and word usage are paramount in a telephone interview. Moreover, the student often must be very assertive to ensure that all of his or her questions are answered. Telephone interviews may be expedient, but they are often as stressful as face-to-face interviews and have significant disadvantages. We *strongly* urge you to do your interviews in-person, if possible, because you will learn more about a potential agency and supervisor during a face-to-face interview. Also, telephone interviews do *not* help to prepare you for the job interviews that lie ahead.

Displaying Professionalism During Internship Interviews

The interview is crucial because it is usually the first time the potential employer has a chance to meet you face-to-face. It is also the primary means for agency personnel to answer crucial questions about you and your abilities. These questions include:

- Do you present a positive, professional image?
- Are you a self-motivated person?
- Do you verbally communicate well?
- Do you have good command of your area of specialization?
- Do you understand yourself?
- Are you knowledgeable about the agency?
- Can you think clearly under pressure?
- Are you patient and tactful?
- Are you a mature person?
- Do you have the right attitude to be an intern with the agency?

Extensive preparation helps to ensure that your interviewer will answer "yes" to many of these questions; however, there are also other important things to keep in mind when you participate in an interview. Here are some of them:

Appearance and Grooming. For an interview, it is *essential* to be neat, clean, and dressed in a professional manner. Select your clothes well in advance of the interview date, and check them carefully for neatness, cleanliness and fit the night before. Be certain no mending is necessary. If you do not have an "eye" for colors and styles, have a knowledgeable friend or relative help you select your interview attire. It is best to stay with traditional, conservative styles in both dress and grooming, and it is better to over-dress than under-dress for an interview. It is important to be relaxed and comfortable during the interview, so wear clothing that helps you feel that way. Also, avoid wearing anything into the interview that might distract you or your interviewer (e.g., a tie that is too "loud" or tied too tightly; too much makeup, perfume, or after shave; excess jewelry).

Confidence and Enthusiasm. From the moment you walk into your interview, you need to let your interviewer know that you have confidence in your abilities and enthusiasm for doing an internship with the agency. First, and foremost, *relax* as you approach the interview situation. Greet everyone you meet with a warm, energetic smile and a positive greeting (e.g., "I've been looking forward to this interview.") If a handshake is appropriate, be sure to offer a firm one. Respond to questions directly and concisely, but be certain to answer them completely. Avoid yes/no responses, one-word answers, and long, rambling responses. Be aware of your pace of speech to assure that it is neither too fast nor too slow. Be sure that your answers demonstrate genuine interest in the agency and its services. Moreover, display confidence that, as an intern, you will be an asset to the agency.

Sincerity. It is essential that your interviewer get to know the "real" you. If you try to act like someone else during an interview, you will probably be perceived as insincere. Rather, just relax and act naturally. If something funny happens, laugh with your interviewer. If you are describing an emotional experience, show a little of your emotion. You want your interviewer to know that you are both professional *and* personable.

Nonverbal Communication. People say a lot about themselves without even opening their mouths. The way they sit or the way they walk tells people how they feel about themselves and others. Research indicates that such nonverbal communication may be as important, and possibly more important, than verbal communication. Let people know you have confidence in yourself by maintaining eye contact with them during the interview. Maintain an upright, but not stiff, posture with just a little forward lean. Acknowledge what others say with a nod, confirming that you are carefully listening to them. Also, attending to their nonverbal communication will help you respond appropriately during the interview.

Concentration and Active Listening. Interviewing takes intense concentration and active listening skills. Attend carefully to what is said to you during the interview. It is embarrassing to ask a question that has already been answered by an interviewer. Also, concentrate intensely on questions that you are asked. If you do not understand a question, it is perfectly acceptable to ask for clarification; however, if you do not *hear* a question, an interviewer may have doubts about your listening skills.

Habits and Mannerisms. Do you have any bad habits or annoying mannerisms that may affect your interviews, such as twisting your hair, playing with jewelry, tapping a pencil or pen, or fidgeting? Habits are things you have learned, and you can eliminate them only through relearning or retraining. The first step toward eliminating these habits is to identify them during your mock interviews. Then, practice your interviewing skills, concentrating on leaving out any bad habits or annoying mannerisms.

Positive Attitude. Agency supervisors like to have student interns who are upbeat and positive in their approach to school, work and life. Be sure that your interview reflects a positive outlook. Avoid making negative or sarcastic statements about your university, or previous employment. If a question requires you to say something negative (e.g., "What do you like least about your previous job?"), try to have your response include positive aspects (e.g., "We did not have a large enough budget to put all of our programming ideas into action").

Promptness. Arriving to an interview on time demonstrates that you are a reliable person who can be counted on. We suggest that you plan to arrive at the facility at least 15 minutes early, but do *not* report to the receptionist until just before the appointment time. Use the extra time to go over information on the agency, review your answers to potential questions, and, if necessary, stop at the restroom.

Nervousness and Mistakes. Despite attempts to relax and display confidence, it is natural to be nervous during an internship interview. Good interviewers understand this, and they won't judge you harshly if you appear a little nervous or make a mistake during the interview. If this happens, feel free to admit your nervousness, take a second to relax and restore your confidence, then continue with the interview. Not getting flustered by nervousness or a mistake demonstrates to an interviewer that you respond well under pressure.

Control. During the interview, it is important to remember that the interviewer is in control. Allow him or her to take the lead. In an interview, it is important not to come across as argumentative, pushy or over-confident. Allowing the interviewer to set the tone and pace of an interview lets him or her know that you understand when *not* to assert yourself. The interviewer also decides how and when to conclude the interview. However, remember that you do need to assert yourself at the end of the interview if all of your questions/concerns have not been addressed.

Conclusion. At the end of the interview, be sure to smile and thank everyone associated with the interview, including the receptionist. Final impressions, like first impressions, tend to be lasting ones.

FOLLOWING-UP AFTER AN INTERVIEW

Yogi Berra is credited with saying, "It's never over 'til it's over." An internship interview is not even over when it appears to be over. You still need to follow-up after the actual interview is complete, including correspondence with your interviewer, self-evaluation, and agency assessment.

Correspondence

If you promised to send additional information (e.g., references, examples of your writing) to the interviewer, be sure to do so immediately after returning to home or school. In addition, it is generally considered good interview etiquette to write a *brief* thank-you letter expressing your appreciation for the interview. This letter also gives you the chance to reemphasize your enthusiasm for the agency's programs and services, and to restate how much you hope to learn during an internship with the agency. Finally, this letter allows you to add any information you may have forgotten to convey during the interview. Be sure to send your thank you letter as soon as possible after the interview. Figures 6.4 and 6.5 provide examples of thank-you letters following face-to-face interviews.

Self-Evaluation

Your follow-up should also include a self-evaluation of your interview performance. To conduct your self-evaluation, first review the information in "Participating in an Interview" on page 115; then answer the following questions:

- Was your physical appearance appropriate? Do you feel you gave the impression of a well-groomed, healthy individual?
- Did you speak clearly, distinctly, and refrain from using inappropriate words such as "yeah," nope," "and-uh," "uhmm" or "aahhh"?
- Were your answers direct, clear and concise? Do you feel they were understood by the interview(s)?
- Were you self-confident, open and at ease in your responses?
- Did you display enthusiasm for the agency and its services?
- What do you feel were your strong points or strengths during the interview?
- What do you feel were your weaknesses, and what steps will you take to improve upon them during future interviews?
- What steps will you take to make the above improvements?
- How would you rate your overall performance?

Figure 6.4
Sample Thank You Letter #1

Date of Typing

Ms. Patricia Lawson, CTRS
Director of Therapeutic Recreation
Marabelle State Hospital
4800 Tennison Road
Bridgewater, CT 06452

Dear Ms. Lawson:

Thank you for taking the time to interview me for an internship position at Marabelle State Hospital. I was extremely impressed with both the facilities at the hospital and your progressive Therapeutic Recreation program.

As you know, my career goal is to be a Certified Therapeutic Recreation Specialist working with persons who have psychological disorders. My visit to Marabelle State Hospital has reaffirmed this goal, and I am excited about the possibility of doing an internship under your supervision.

During the interview, you requested that I send you a sample of my writing. Enclosed is a copy of a paper I wrote entitled "Leisure Education for Persons with Addictive Disorders." This paper was written last semester for REC 479 (Issues and Trends in Therapeutic Recreation).

Thank you again for the interview, and I look forward to hearing from you soon.

Sincerely,

Betty Jean Tearney
34 Rennie Way
Storrs, CT 06268
(203) 497-2874

Figure 6.5
Sample Thank You Letter #2

---

143 Hartswick Ave.
Tallahassee, FL 31532
(904) 322-1794

Date of Typing

Mr. Terrance Brown
Golf Professional
Liberty Golf Club and Resort
Golf Club Lane
Sunnydale, FL 33179

Dear Mr. Brown:

I enjoyed meeting you last Thursday, and appreciate your interviewing me for an internship position at Liberty Golf Club and Resort. I especially want to thank you for providing me with an extensive tour of your impressive facilities.

During the interview, you expressed interest in knowing more about New Venture Country Club in New Orleans, where my parents are members. Enclosed is an informational brochure on New Venture. David Shank, New Venture's teaching professional, requested that you call him if you want additional information on the club.

Once again, thank you for the interview and tour. I look forward to hearing from you as soon as a decision is made regarding the internship position.

Sincerely,

Jean Broussard

Enclosure

Agency Assessment

In addition to evaluating your performance during the interview, you also need to assess whether the interview revealed any new information about the agency and its services. Pay particular attention to the interviewer's answers to important questions you asked during the interview (see Figure 6.3, page 114). Then ask yourself, "Do I still feel that this agency will help me meet my educational and career goals?" If the answer is "No," eliminate this agency from consideration and continue your internship search. If the answer is "Yes," this agency should be considered when you make your final internship placement decision (Chapter Seven).

SUMMARY

All the work you have done up to this point has led to the interview. An internship interview is a two-way process that provides information to both the interviewer and you. This chapter has assisted you in identifying areas you need to consider and practice before entering through your interviewer's doors. If you prepare carefully and thoroughly, you will be able to give your best effort throughout the interview process. Hopefully, your interviews will lead to one or more internship offers. Then, all that remains is for you to make your final decision. The next chapter will help prepare you for making that decision.

CHAPTER SEVEN

Selection and Final Planning

"Life is either a daring adventure or nothing at all."
—Helen Keller

Following your internship interviews, if all went well, you should have more than one internship offer to consider. It is now time to select the agency that best meets your academic, professional and personal needs. Sometimes the choice is obvious because one agency's internship program is ideal for your academic needs and future direction. Often, however, the choice is neither obvious nor easy to make.

This chapter will help you to:

• Organize your thoughts in order to select
the best internship agency for *you*.;

• Assist you with how to notify agencies of your selection; and

• Help you to plan for your internship experience.

Making Your Selection

Many times, students who have received more than one internship offer will ask for help in making their selection. Although you *should* seek information from friends, relatives, and faculty members, remember that the final selection is up to you. In fact, the exercises in this manual, plus your interviews, have provided the information you need to make your final agency selection. If you are having trouble deciding which agency is best for you, answering the following questions will help.

If I did my internship at (*name of agency*), would I be able to :

(1)   Refine and acquire professional skills important to my career (see Figure 1.3, page 10)?

(2)   Do the type of work I enjoy most (see Figure 2.1, page 16)?

(3)   Gain experience in the kind of professional position I ultimately want to have (see Figure 2.1, page 16 and 2.3, page 26)?

(4)   Meet my internship goals (see Figure 2.2, page 24)?

(5)   Meet my most important internship needs and preferences (see Figure 3.3, page 38)?

(6)   Feel comfortable working with the people I met during my interview?

EXERCISE TIME!

After answering these questions, does one agency stand out by meeting the criteria that are most important to *you*? If so, your choice should be easy. If not, complete the Internship Agency Evaluation Form (Figure 7.1) on the following three pages. By listing the pros and cons of each agency, your decision will be easier to make.

Figure 7.1
Internship Agency Evaluation Form (Agency #1)

Take some time to identify the pros and cons of doing an internship with the following agency. Then, compare this list with the pros and cons offered by other agencies you are considering. This comparison will help you decide which agency offers you the best internship.

Name of Agency _____

PROS	CONS

Figure 7.1 (Continued)
Internship Agency Evaluation Form (Agency #2)

Name of Agency _____

PROS	CONS

Figure 7.1 (Continued)
Internship Agency Evaluation Form (Agency #3)

Name of Agency _____

PROS	CONS

Your internship agency selection is *very* important to your professional career, so take your time. Consult with others, consider all of the information above, and select the agency that offers you the best possible internship.

Notification of Selection

Once you have made your selection, you need to communicate your intentions to all agencies with which you interviewed. First, if you do not have your offer in writing, telephone your first choice agency and confirm the offer. Let appropriate agency personnel know that you appreciate being selected and tell them you plan to accept. You should also confirm important information at this time, such as pay or stipend, work responsibilities, starting date, and length of internship. Then, write an acceptance letter confirming your selection, expressing your excitement about the internship, and confirming important information. Figure 7.2 (page 129) provides an example of an acceptance letter.

After you have confirmed your selection with your internship agency, you need to notify other agencies that you will not be doing your internship with them. Even if you notify them by telephone, you should send a letter thanking them for their consideration and explaining your decision. This is often a difficult letter to write, but it is very important. Sending a well-written letter that declines an internship will demonstrate your professionalism and keep your options open for future employment with each agency. Figure 7.3 (page 130) provides an example of a letter declining an internship.

Figure 7.2
Sample Acceptance Letter

Date of Typing

Ms. Patricia Lawson, CTRS
Director of Therapeutic Recreation
Marabelle State Hospital
4800 Tennison Road
Bridgewater, CT 06452

Dear Ms. Lawson:

I am pleased to accept your offer of an internship in Therapeutic Recreation at Marabelle State Hospital. After visiting your facility in March, I knew that your program was ideally suited to my professional interests, and I am very excited about the learning opportunities available to me.

As I mentioned during our phone conversation, my internship is scheduled to begin on May 6th and end on August 5th. It is my understanding that I will work 40 hours per week, and that Mr. Thomas Calloway, CTRS, will be my direct supervisor. I enjoyed meeting Tom during my visit, and look forward to learning from him.

Thank you for offering me an internship with your program, and I look forward to seeing you in May.

Sincerely,

Betty Jean Tearney
34 Rennie Way
Storrs, CT 06268
(203) 497-2874

Figure 7.3
Sample Letter of Decline

---

143 Hartswick Ave.
Tallahassee, FL 31532
(904) 322-1794

Date of Typing

Mr. Terrance Brown
Golf Professional
Liberty Golf Club and Resort
Golf Club Lane
Sunnydale, FL 33179

Dear Mr. Brown:

Thank you for your offer of an internship at Liberty Golf Club and Resort. As you know, I was very impressed with your operation, and enjoyed meeting you and your excellent staff.

I am certain that an internship under your supervision would be a valuable learning experience for any student. However, I must decline your generous offer. After careful consideration, I have decided to do my internship at New Venture Country Club in New Orleans. As you know New Venture is near my home and offers an internship program that is ideal for meeting my academic and career goals.

Thank you for your consideration and for the courtesy that you and your staff extended to me. Perhaps we will have the opportunity to work together in the future.

Sincerely,

Jean Broussard

Planning for Your Internship

Getting ready for your internship is exciting, but it also involves hard work and thorough planning. This is especially true if you select an internship agency that is distant from your home or school. The following information is intended to help plan for your internship experience.

Communication

It is vital for you to establish and maintain good communication with your agency supervisor and university faculty. Any problems, concerns, or changes in plans need to be clearly communicated to appropriate personnel. Research has demonstrated that communication is the single most important element in a successful internship experience.

Expenses

Be sure to assess how much it will cost you to live at your internship site, and plan your finances carefully. Some agencies, for example, provide free food or housing for interns, but others require that interns pay for everything. Also, transportation costs are sometimes covered by agencies, but generally they are the intern's responsibility.

Attire

Proper dress depends largely upon the type of agency you select and the nature of your duties. Think back on your interview, visualize the clothing worn by agency staff and interns, and plan to dress accordingly. You should also check with your agency supervisor, in advance, to determine if there are special clothing requirements for interns. If you are moving away from school or home, be sure to plan clothing for both work and recreation.

Orientation

Prior to arriving for the first day of your internship, review promotional materials and all information you have collected about the agency. It may prove embarrassing if you have forgotten some important details about the agency, its services, and its rules and regulations.

Resources and References

While in school, you have probably accumulated a large amount of materials that will prove helpful during your internship. Select the most important ones and be sure to take them with you. Textbooks, course notes, resource files, and professional journals may be extremely useful to both you and your supervisor. If your internship is away from home or school, remember to take important phone numbers with you, too.

Time Management

Punctuality and promptness are valuable assets for any professional, including interns. A few items are extremely helpful in using your time wisely, including (1) a reliable watch, (2) a good alarm clock, and (3) a schedule book or daily planner. Be sure you have all three while on your internship.

Supplies and Equipment

Be sure to take or have access to supplies and equipment that are important for your internship responsibilities. Depending on your duties or assignments, one or more of the following may prove helpful: calculator, personal computer, typewriter, tape recorder, art supplies, drafting tools, and sports equipment.

SUMMARY

This final chapter is designed to help you select your internship agency. By carefully evaluating your choices, you will be able select the best possible internship for *you*. Once this decision is made, you need to communicate your choice in a professional manner, including writing letters to the agency you selected and to the ones you declined. Finally, you should prepare for your internship by thoroughly planning for your needs. By selecting your agency wisely and planning thoroughly, you will assure yourself of a successful internship experience.

FINAL COMMENT FROM AUTHORS

Congratulations on completing this manual, and we hope that it has been helpful to you! Although intended primarily as a guide to internships, this manual is also a valuable resource for finding employment in recreation and leisure services. The skills needed to find and apply for an internship are essentially the same as finding and applying for a job. Thus, the information, exercises, and resources in this manual should prove helpful to you as you approach graduation and seek a full-time job in the field. If you have any suggestions to improve this manual or would like to provide information for future updates, please send them to:

Edward E. Seagle Jr., Ed.D.
Department of Recreation & Parks Management
California State University, Chico
Chico, CA 95929-0560

REFERENCE MATERIALS

This section provides a list of directories and other materials that may help you in your internship search process. Some of these materials are available in public and university libraries, but others will need to be ordered from the addresses provided. Call or write first to see if the item is available free or for a nominal charge. Before ordering items that cost a lot of money, you should first check to see if they are available from your internship coordinator or other faculty members, leisure service professionals, and state or local professional organizations. Also, you might call the publishers of membership directories—they may be willing to give you the names of members near your home or school. Some items may *only* be available through your university's internship coordinator (e.g., Army Summer Recreation Internship Program).

Job bulletins have been included with these resources because they often list internships, and because they may be valuable resources for you after graduation. Before ordering any job bulletin, we recommend you examine a sample copy. If your university does not subscribe, you should call or write for a complimentary issue (even if it is an outdated issue) *before* subscribing. Many state recreation and park societies or associations have their own job bulletins, so we suggest checking with the state society or association in your area (see Appendix B) to see if they provide internship or job information.

The following reference materials are organized according to interest areas. However, the first section includes resources that should be of interest to everyone because they list a variety of agencies that may offer internships. The remaining sections are limited to specialized resources (e.g., Commercial Recreation, Community Recreation, Military Recreation, Outdoor Recreation, and Therapeutic Recreation).

General Recreation and Leisure Resources

Title: Employ

Source: National Recreation and Park Association
2775 South Quincy Street, Suite 300
Arlington, VA 22206
Phone: (703) 820-4940

Comments: Nine issues annually with useful information on job search in recreation and leisure field. Sometimes includes additional resources (i.e., October/November 1989 lists associations and organizations in Commercial Recreation).

Title: Job Bulletin

Source: Leisure Studies Office
                S-203 Henderson Building
                School of Hotel, Restaurant and Recreation Management
                Penn State University
                University Park, PA 16802
                Phone: (814) 865-1851

Comments: Periodic nationwide listing of jobs and internships in recreation and leisure.
                Subscription fee required.

Title: Job Opportunities Bulletin

Source: University of Illinois at Urbana-Champaign
                Department of Leisure Studies
                104 Huff Hall
                1206 S. Fourth Street
                Champaign, IL 61820
                Phone: (217) 333-1824

Comments: Periodic nationwide listing of jobs and internships in recreation and leisure.
                Subscription fee required.

Title: Job or Employment Opportunities Bulletin

Source: Some state recreation and park societies/associations,
                see Appendix B for names and addresses.

Comments: Periodic nationwide listing of jobs and internships in recreation and leisure.
                Subscription fees generally required.

Title: NRPA Student Branch Internship Directory

Source: National Recreation and Park Association
                Attn: Student Branch
                2775 South Quincy Street, Suite 300
                Arlington, VA 22206
                Phone: (703) 578-5547

Comments: Lists approximately 200 agencies offering internships in recreation and leisure
                services. Updated every other year, this directory gives details on internships,
                including salaries or stipends. Cost: $7.50 for NRPA members; $15.00 for nonmembers.

Title: National Directory of Internships

Source: National Society for Internships and Experiential Education
3509 Haworth Drive, Suite 207
Raleigh, NC 27609
Phone: (919) 787-3263

Comments: Nationwide directory of internship opportunities in a variety of professional fields. Organized by type of organization, including environment, government, health, human interest, and women's issues.

Title: NESRA Membership and Peer Network Directory

Source: National Employee Services and Recreation Association
2400 South Downing Avenue
Westchester, IL 60154

Comments: Nationwide list of members, including place of employment. Should be of particular interest to students in commercial recreation and community recreation (program services).

Title: Parks and Recreation Opportunities Job Bulletin

Source: National Recreation and Park Association
2775 South Quincy Street, Suite 300
Arlington, VA 22206
Phone: (703) 820-4940

Comments: Periodic listing of jobs, internships, and educational opportunities in recreation and leisure. Subscription fee required.

Title: Y National Vacancy List

Source: YMCA of the USA
101 North Wacker Drive
Chicago, IL 60606
Phone: (312) 977-0031 or (800) 872-9622

Comments: Periodic publication informing subscribers of YMCA professional vacancies throughout the U.S.

Title: AAHPERD Update Job Exchange

Source: American Alliance for Health, Physical Education,
                  Recreation and Dance
                  1900 Association Drive
                  Reston, VA 22091-8006
                  Phone: (703) 476-3484; FAX: (703) 476-9527

Comments: Included in periodic newsletter (Update) published by AAHPERD.
                   Free to association members (student memberships available).

Commercial Recreation

Title: Business DIALOG

Source: DIALOG Information Services
                 3460 Hillview Avenue
                 Palo Alto, CA 94304
                 Phone: (800) 3-DIALOG

Comments: On-line database for obtaining background information on recreation businesses.
                  Expensive fees, but targeted search is available through many public libraries.

Title: Club Business International

Source: IRSA
                 132 Brookline Avenue
                 Boston, MA 02215
                 Phone: (617) 236-1500

Comments: Monthly magazine concerned with racquet and fitness clubs.
                   Has "Marketplace" section listing job opportunities.
                   Copies may be available at your local racquet and fitness clubs.

Title: Hotel and Travel Index

Source: Your local hotels or libraries.

Comments: *Hugh* document, including national and international listings of hotels, motels, and
                   resorts. Includes advertisements providing details on some properties.

Title: *Jobs in paradise: The definitive guide to exotic jobs everywhere*
                by Jeffrey Maltzman

Source: Harper Collins Publishers
                10 East 53rd Street
                New york, NY 10022
                Phone: (212) 207-7000

Comments: Published in 1990 this book contains a wealth of information on part-time
                and summer jobs that may be appropriate for internships.
                Available in many libraries.

Title: Job Placement Service Bulletin

Source: Resort and Commercial Recreation Association
                P.O. Box 1208
                New Port Richey, FL 34656-1208
                Phone: (813) 845-7373

Comments: Monthly bulletin listing jobs and internships in Commercial Recreation
                throughout the United States. Subscription fee required.

Title: Meeting News Directory

Source: Meeting News, Circulation Department
                Room 3201
                1515 Broadway
                New York, NY 10036

Comments: Extensive lising of resort hotels and recreation service industry.
                Written primarily for meeting planners.

Title: NTA Tour Operator Directory

Source: National Tour Association, Inc.
                North American Headquarters
                P.O. Box 3071
                Lexington, KY 40596-3071
                Phone: (800) NTA-8886

Comments: Nationwide list of all NTA Tour Operator members.

Title: PCMA Membership Directory

Source: Professional Convention Management Association
                100 Vestavia Office Park, Suite 220
                Birmingham, AL 35216
                Phone: (205) 823-7262

Comments: Nationwide list of member, associations, and affiliating organizations.

Title: Placement Service Newsletter

Source: Philadelphia Chapter of the Public Relations Society of America
                Department of Journalism
                Temple University
                Philadelphia, PA 19122
                Phone: (215) 787-8757

Comments: Eleven issues annually with jobs in marketing and public relations.
                Most listings are for jobs in Philadelphia and surrounding states.
                Subscription fee required. The Public Relations Society of America
                is a national organization with chapters throughout the country.

Title: RCRA Membership Directory

Source: Resort and Commercial Recreation Association
                P.O. Box 1208
                New Port Richey, FL 34656-1208
                Phone: (813) 845-7373

Comments: Nationwide list of members, including title and place of employment.

Title: The Official Directory of Festivals, Sports and Special Events

Source: International Events Group
                213 West Institute Place, Suite 303
                Chicago, IL 60610
                Phone: (312) 944-1727

Comments: Listing of events, including sponsors.

Title: Sports Advantage

Source: Standard Rate and Data Service
             3004 Glenview Road
             Wilmette, IL 60091
             Phone: (708) 441-2345

Comments: Extensive listing of commercial recreation and sports marketing corporate
             sponsorship. Two volume series, updated yearly.

Title: Sports Marketplace

Source: Sportsguide
             P.O. Box 1417
             Princeton, NJ 08542
             Phone: (609) 921-8599

Comments: Includes major sports and recreation production firms, plus
             corporate sponsorship programs.

Community Recreation —see General Recreation and Leisure Resources (above)

Military Recreation

Title: Army Summer Recreation Internship Program

Source: Army Community Recreation Directorate
             CFSC-CR-RO
             Alexandria, VA 22331-0510
             Phone: (703) 325-2523

Comments: Annual list of national and international internship opportunities
             with the U.S. Army.

Title: Job Opportunities Bulletin

Source: Bureau of Naval Personnel Detachment
             Navy Morale, Welfare and Recreation Training Unit
             Building 1489
             Naval Air Station
             Patuxent River, MD 20670-5489

Comments: Monthly listing of jobs (nationwide) in Navy MWR programs.

Title: NMPC Morale, Welfare and Recreation Activities

Source: Department of the Navy
                Naval Military Personnel Command
                Washington, DC 20370-5000
                Phone: (703) 746-6533

Comments: Booklet containing nationwide master list of phone numbers and
                addresses of Navy MWR activities.

Title: Resource Sharing: Recreation Intern Programs within the Armed Forces

Source: Armed Forces Recreation Society
                National Recreation and Park Association
                2775 South Quincy Street, Suite 300
                Arlington, VA 22206
                Phone: (703) 820-4940

Comments: Booklet with guidelines and information on internships with the
                United States Air Force, Army, and Navy.

Title: U. S. Navy MWR Intern News

Source: Bureau of Naval Personnel Detachment
                Navy Morale, Welfare and Recreation Training Unit
                Building 1489
                Naval Air Station
                Patuxent River, MD 20670-5489
                Phone: (301) 863-3861

Comments: Seasonal list of Navy internship opportunities, plus other useful
                information on securing an internship with the Navy.

Outdoor Recreation

Title: Connections

Source: The CEIP Fund, Inc.
                286 Congress Street
                Boston, MA 02210
                Phone: (617) 426-4375

Comments: Newsletter containing information on career opportunities and internships in
                environment-related agencies. The CEIP Fund was formerly known as the
                Center for Environmental Internship Programs. Also sponsors annual career
                conference. The CEIP Fund also sponsors an annual career conference.

Title: Conservation Directory

Source: National Wildlife Federation
               1400 Sixteenth Street, N.W.
               Washington, DC 20036-2266
               Phone: (202) 797-6800

Comments: Nationwide list of organizations, agencies and officials concerned with natural
               resource use and management.

Title: Guide to Accredited Camps

Source: American Camping Association
               5000 State Road 67 North
               Martinsville, IN 46151-7902
               Phone: (800) 428-2267

Comments: Nationwide directory of accredited camps.

Title: Internships and Summer Jobs at Public Gardens

Source: American Association of Botanical Gardens and Arboreta
               P.O. Box 206
               Swarthmore, PA 19081

Comments: Nationwide listing of opportunities in horticulture.

Title: Job Scan

Source: Student Conservation Association, Inc.
               Attn: Linda Rounds, Editor
               P. O. Box 550
               Charlestown, NH 03603
               Phone: (603) 826-7732

Comments: National monthly listing of environmental and natural resource management jobs.
               Paid subscription required.

Title: The Job's Clearinghouse

Source: Association for Experiential Education
                Campus Box 249
                Boulder, CO 80309
                Phone: (303) 492-1547

Comments: Nationwide list of jobs in experiential education programs.
                Paid subscription required.

Title: Park Law Enforcement Agency Directory

Source: Dr. James Stribling
                Extension Recreation and Park Specialist
                Texas Agricultural Extension Service
                The Texas A & M University
                212 Francis Hall
                College Station, TX 77843-2261
                Phone: (409) 845-5418

Comments: Nationwide listing of park law enforcement agencies.

Title: Volunteer Positions

Source: Resource Assistance Program
                Student Conservation Association, Inc.
                P. O. Box 550
                Charlestown, NH 03603
                Phone: (603) 826-4301

Comments: Listing of volunteer seasonal staff positions at resource management
                agencies throughout the United States.

Therapeutic Recreation

Title: Employment Update

Source: American Therapeutic Recreation Association
                P. O. Box 15215
                Hattiesburg, MS 39404-5215
                Phone: (800) 553-0304

Comments: Periodic list of jobs and internships in therapeutic recreation
                throughout the United States. Distributed free to ATRA members.

STATE RECREATION AND PARKS
SOCIETIES/ASSOCIATIONS

Many of the following state societies/associations have job referral services and provide technical assistance to students, including assistance with identifying potential internship agencies. This list is limited to National Recreation and Park Association affiliates with executive directors. If you are interested in the address of a state society/association not listed below, contact the NRPA Great Lakes Regional Office (see last section of list).

Alabama Recreation and Park Society
P.O. Box 4744
Montgomery, AL 36103-4744
(205) 832-4555

Arizona Parks and Recreation Association
3124 East Roosevelt
Phoenix, AZ 85008
(602) 267-7246

California Park and Recreation Society
3031 F. Street, Suite 202
Sacramento, CA 95816
(916) 446-2777

Colorado Parks and Recreation Association
P.O. Box 1037
Wheat Ridge, CO 80034
(303) 231-0943

Connecticut Recreation and Park Association
15 Gilead Street
Hebron, CT 06248
(203) 288-9406

Florida Recreation and Park Association
411 Office Plaza Drive
Tallahassee, FL 32301
(904) 878-3221

Georgia Recreation and Park Association
1285 Parker Road, SE
Conyers, GA 30207-5957
(404) 760-1403

Illinois Association of Park Districts
211 East Monroe
Springfield, IL 62701
(217) 523-4554

Illinois Park and Recreation Association
1N141 County Farm Road, Suite 100
Winfield, IL 60190-2023
(708) 752-0141

Indiana Park and Recreation Association
101 Hurricane Street
Franklin, IN 46131
(317) 736-8994

Iowa Park and Recreation Association
203 Fieldhouse
University of Iowa
Iowa City, IA 52242
(319) 335-9351

Kansas Recreation and Park Association
700 Jackson Street, Suite 705
Topeka, KS 66603-3731
(913) 235-6533

Kentucky Recreation and Park Society
200 High Street
Bowling Green, KY 42101
(502) 782-7275

Louisiana Recreation and Park Association
P.O. Drawer 14589
Baton Rouge, LA 70808
(504) 927-5134

Maryland Recreation and Park Association
201 Gun Road
Baltimore, MD 21227-3820
(410) 536-4400

Massachusetts Recreation and Park Association
P.O. Box 5135
Conchituate, MA 01778
(508) 650-1126

Michigan Recreation and Park Association
2722 East Michigan, Suite 201
Lansing, MI 48912
(517) 485-9888

Minnesota Recreation and Park Association
5005 West 36th Street
St. Louis Park, MN 55416-2661
(612) 920-6906

Mississippi Recreation and Park Association
P.O. Box 16451
Hattiesburg, MS 39404-6451
(601) 264-3337

Missouri Park and Recreation Association
1203 Missouri Boulevard
Jefferson City, MO 65109
(314) 636-3828

New Jersey Recreation and Park Association
2 Griggstown Causeway
Princeton, NJ 08540
(908) 281-9212

New York State Recreation and Park Society
119 Washington Avenue
Albany, NY 12210
(518) 463-1232

North Carolina Recreation and Park Society
883 Washington Street, #A
Raleigh, NC 27605-3251
(919) 832-5868

Ohio Parks and Recreation Association
420 West Whittier Street
Columbus, OH 43215
(614) 443-2322

Oklahoma Recreation and Park Society
Box 13116
Oklahoma City, OK 73113
(405) 752-0214

Pennsylvania Recreation and Park Society
723 South Atherton Street
State College, PA 16801-4629
(814) 234-4272

South Carolina Recreation and Parks Association
P.O. Box 8453
Columbia, SC 29202-8453
(803) 256-8700

Tennessee Recreation and Parks Association and
    Educational Foundation
2704 12th Avenue South
Nashville, TN 37204
(615) 742-6568

Texas Recreation and Park Society
508 West 12th Street
Austin, TX 78701-1819
(512) 478-7781

Virginia Recreation and Park Society
Route 4, Box 155
Mechanicsville, VA 23111
(804) 730-9447

Washington Recreation and Park Association
350 South 333rd Street
Federal Way, WA 98003
(206) 874-1283

Wisconsin Park and Recreation Association
7000 Greenway, Suite 201
Greendale, WI 53129
(414) 423-1210

National and Regional Offices of NRPA

National Recreation and Park Association (NRPA)
Dean Tice
Executive Director
2775 South Quincy Street, Suite 300
Arlington, VA 22306
(703) 820-4940

NRPA Great Lakes Regional Office
Walter Johnson
Regional Director
650 West Higgins Road
Hoffman Estates, IL 60195
(708) 843-7529

NRPA Northeast Regional Office
Kathy Bartlett
Regional Director
1800 Silas Deane Highway, Suite 1
Rocky Hill, CT 06067
(203) 721-1055

NRPA Pacific Regional Office
Pamela Earle
Regional Director
1600 Sacramento Inn Way, Suite 121
Sacramento, CA 95815
(916) 646-9050

NRPA Southeast Regional Office
Tom Martin
Executive Director
1285 Parker Road, SE
Conyers, GA 30207-5957
(404) 760-1668

NRPA Western Regional Office
Frank Cosgrove
Regional Director
P.O. Box 6900
Colorado Springs, CO 80934
(303) 632-7031

NATIONAL ASSOCIATIONS AND ORGANIZATIONS

The following list includes national organizations that are related to recreation and leisure services. Student memberships are often available at reduced rates, and internship (and employment) information is sometimes available at little or no extra charge. You should contact the organizations that interest you to determine what services they provide to student members.

*For information on additional national and international organizations, we suggest you consult the *Encyclopedia of Associations*, an annual publication of Gale Research Company, Detroit, MI. This publication is available in the reference section of most university libraries.

Aerobics and Fitness Association of America
15250 Ventura Boulevard
Suite 310
Sherman Oaks, CA 91403-3201
(800) 445-5950

American Association of Botanical Gardens and
    Arboreta
786 Church Road
Wayne, PA 19087
(215) 688-1120

American Association of Museums
1225 I. Street N.W.
Washington, DC 20005
(202) 289-1818

American Association for Recreation and Leisure
American Alliance of Health, Physical Education,
Recreation and Dance
1900 Association Drive
Reston, VA 22091
(703) 476-3400

American Camping Association
5000 State Road 67 North
Martinsville, IN 46151-7902
(317) 342-8456

American Therapeutic Recreation Association
P.O. Box 15215
Hattiesburg, MS 39404-5215
(800) 553-0304

Armed Forces Recreation Society
National Recreation and Park Association
2775 South Quincy Street, Suite 300
Arlington, VA 22206
(703) 820-4940

Association for Experiential Education
Campus Box 249
University of Colorado
Boulder, CO 80309
(303) 492-1547

Association for Fitness in Business
342 Massachusetts Avenue, Suite 200
Indianapolis, IN 46204
(317) 636-6621

Association of Nature Center Administrators
P.O. Box 2466
Lodi, CA 95241
(209) 368-7390

Association of Physical Fitness Centers
600 Jefferson Street
Suite 202
Rockville, MD 20852
(301) 424-7744

Club Managers Association of America
1733 King Street
Alexandria, VA 22314
(703) 739-9500

International Association of Amusement Parks and
    Attractions (IAAPA)
1448 Duke Street
Alexandria, VA 22314
(703) 836-4800

IDEA, Inc. (International Dance Exercise
    Association)
6190 Cornerstone Court East, Suite 204
San Diego, CA 92121-3773
(619) 535-8979

International Racquet Sports Association
253 Summer Street
Boston, MA 02210
(617) 951-0055

International Spa and Fitness Association
6935 Wisconsin Avenue
Chevy Chase, MD 20815
(301) 654-8595

National Association for Interpretation
P.O. Box 1892
Fort Collins, CO 80522
(303) 491-6434

National Campground Owners Association
11307 Sunset Hills Road, Suite B-7
Reston, VA 22090
(703) 471-0143

National Council for Therapeutic Recreation
    Certification (NCTRC)
49 South Main Street
Suite 001
Spring Valley, NY 10977-5635
Note: NCTRC is a certifying organization.
(914) 356-9660

National Employee Services and Recreation
    Association
2400 South Downing Avenue
Westchester, IL 60154-5199
(708) 562-8130

National Intramural-Recreational Sports Association
850 S.W. 15th Street
Corvattis, OR 97333-4145
(503) 737-2088

National Recreation and Park Association
2775 South Quincy Street, Suite 300
Arlington, VA 22206
(703) 820-4940

National Strength and Conditioning Association
P.O. Box 81410
Lincoln, NE 68501-1410
(402) 472-3000

National Therapeutic Recreation Society
National Recreation and Park Association
2775 South Quincy Street, Suite 300
Arlington, VA 22206
(703) 820-4940

National Wildlife Federation
1400 Sixteenth Street, N.W.
Washington, DC 20036-2266
(202) 797-6800

Resort and Commercial Recreation Association
P.O. Box 1208
New Port Richey, FL 34656-1208
(813) 845-7373

Student Conservation Association, Inc.
P.O. Box 550
Charlestown, NH 03603
(603) 826-4301

RECOMMENDED READINGS

Books and Manuals

Bloomberg, G., and Holden, M. (1991). *The women's job search handbook.* Charlotte, VT: Williamson.

Bolles, R. N. (Updated Annually). *What color is your parachute?* Berkeley, CA: Ten Speed Press.

Bullis, M., and Watson, D. (1986). *Career education of hearing impaired students.* New York, NY: Rehabilitation Research and Training Center.

Elsa, J. G. (1984). *First impression best impression.* New York, NY: Simon & Schuster, Inc.

Good, C. (1990). *Does your resume wear combat boots?* Charlottesville, VA: Word Store.

Greenhaus, J. H. (1987). *Career management.* New York, NY: CBS College Publishing.

Figler, H. (1988). *The complete job-search handbook.* New York, NY: Henry Holt & Co.

Hizer, D. V., and Rosenberg, A. D. (1985). *The resume handbook.* Boston, MA: Bob Adams, Inc.

Hopkins-Best, M. S., and Yurcisin, A. (1988). *Reaching the hidden majority: A leader's guide to career preparation for disabled women and girls.* Cranston, RI: Carroll Press.

Jackson, T. (1978). *Guerilla tactics in the job market: A practical manual.* New York, NY: Bantam Books.

Krannich, R. L., and Krannich, C. R. (1990). *The complete guide to public employment.* Woodbridge, VA: Impact.

Levering, R. (1988). *A great place to work.* New York, NY: Avon Books.

Marks, J. E., and Lewis, A. (1983). *Job hunting for the disabled: A search for dignity.* Woodbury, NY: Barron's Educational Series, Inc.

McGee-Cooper, A. (1990). *You don't have to go home from work exhausted.* Dallas, TX: Bowen & Rogers.

Medley, H. A. (1984). *Sweaty palms: The neglected art of being interviewed.* Berkeley, CA: Ten Speed Press.

Molloy, J. T. (1989). *New dress for success.* New York, NY: Warner Books.

Murphy, K. J. (1991). *Surviving the cut: An executive's guide to successful job hunting in today's tough market.* New York, NY: Bantam Books.

Pettus, T. (1981). *One on one, win the interview, win the job.* New York, NY: Random House.

Powell, C. R. (1991). *Career planning today.* Dubuque, IA: Kendall/Hunt.

Rush. H. L. (1991). *Job Search: The complete manual for job seekers.* New York, NY: American Management Association.

Shertzer, B. (1985). *Career planning*: *Freedom to choose*. Boston, MA: Houghton-Mifflin.

Waitely, D., and Witt, R. L. (1985). *The joy of working*. New York, NY: Dodd, Mead & Company

Wallach, E. J., and Arnold, P. (1984). *The job search companion*: *The organizer for job seekers*. Cambridge, MA: Harvard Common Press.

Wegmann, R., Chapman, R., and Johnson, M. (1989). *Looking for work in the new economy*. Salt Lake City, UT: Olympus.

Yates, M. J. (1990). *Knock 'em dead with great answers to tough interview questions*. Boston, MA: Bob Adams, Inc.

Yates, M. J. (1990). *Resumes that knock 'em dead*. Boston, MA: Bob Adams, Inc.

Periodicals

Career Futures. Westport, CT: Career Information Services.

Career Placement Manuals. Chicago, IL: CRS Recruitment Publications.

Careers and the Disabled. Greenlawn, NY: Equal Opportunity Publications.

CPC Annual. Bethlehem, PA: College Placement Council.

Employ. Arlington, VA: National Recreation and Park Association.

Journal of Employment Counseling. Columbia, MO: American Personnel and Guidance Association.

Journal of College Placement. Bethlehem, PA: College Placement Council.

The Black Collegian. New Orleans, LA: Black Collegian Service.